The ADVISER

Herbert Goldhamer

Elsevier · New York
NEW YORK · OXFORD · SHANNON

ELSEVIER NORTH-HOLLAND, INC.
52 Vanderbilt Avenue, New York, New York 10017

Distributors outside the United States and Canada:
Thomond Books
(A Division of Elsevier/North-Holland
Scientific Publishers, Ltd)
P.O. Box 85
Limerick, Ireland

Library of Congress Cataloging in Publication Data

Goldhamer, Herbert, 1907–1977
The adviser.

Bibliography: p. 170
Includes index.
1. Government consultants. I. Title.
JF1525. C6G64 350 77-10728
ISBN 0-444-99040-2

Manufactured in the United States of America

Designed by Loretta Li

To Jody

Contents

Preface

The advisers to political leaders do not lack for attention in contemporary political journalism, in political biography, and in memoirs. In addition, a substantial literature now exists on the role of the expert and adviser in government service in the United States and Great Britain during and after World War II. Oddly enough, however, there is, to my knowledge, no work on the adviser that covers a sufficient range of periods and cultures to throw into relief the continuities and diversities of this political figure over the centuries in which he has played his important role in politics. The present essay contributes toward such a work by isolating a set of themes for the analysis of the political adviser and by illustrating, if only briefly, the diverse forms these themes have taken over the approximately four millennia during which we have had a recorded literature and history dealing with political life. The political adviser appears in man's earliest surviving documents and has never disappeared from the political stage since that time. Surely, this figure deserves more systematic attention than he has received.

The reader will understand that a brief essay of such broad scope must confine itself, in dealing with individual points, to a very limited number of illustrations. Both for purposes of succinctness and in order to convey something of the personality and style of the political figures with whom I deal, I have preferred in many instances to express their views by direct quotations from their writings or from those who were close observers of them. I see no purpose in saying in three or four sentences of paraphrase what Francis Bacon said with infinitely greater grace and acuteness in one or two sentences. I have permitted myself relatively rapid transitions from illustration to illustration and from point to point. This *pointilliste* mode of exposition contributes greatly to conciseness and has enabled me to cover a lot more ground than this slim volume might suggest. It is, I believe, appropriate to an essay where I am principally concerned to distinguish a number of important themes deserving more detailed study.

I am indebted to The Rand Graduate Institute and its director Charles Wolf, Jr., for enabling me to devote time to the preparation of this book. I am indebted, too, to Jascha Kessler, Nathan Leites, and Hans Speier who read the entire manuscript and made many valuable suggestions. Andrew W. Marshall and Paul Hammond brought their experience in government to bear on several points that have benefited from their comments. I owe a great debt to my wife who patiently checked elusive references, guided the work through all the stages from rough manuscript to final typescript and to publisher's proofs, and above all was an invaluable critic. Still, having exercised my prerogative as author to have the last word, I must absolve all those who helped me from responsibility for any errors. Finally, I am grateful to Twylah Lawson not only for preparing the typescript but also for the speed and good humor with which this was accomplished.

HERBERT GOLDHAMER

His death on August 8, 1977 deprived the author of the opportunity to review his manuscript in printed form. I have taken the liberty of making some minor changes in the interest of consistency or to correct errors brought to light in the proofs, but the present text was denied the polishing I know it would have received had the author himself been able to see the manuscript through its final stages.

J.G.

There are in All-under-Heaven three truths: First, that even wise men find unattainable tasks; second, that even strong men find immovable objects; and third, that even brave men find invincible opponents.

—HAN FEI TZU

The ADVISER

Introduction

The term 'adviser' lacks, both in political practice and in political studies, a well-established meaning. This stems from the unofficial status of many advisers and the greater variety of their roles as compared with political officers whose powers have been well defined by law or custom. It is not self-evident, then, who is to be included as an adviser, especially when the term is used—as in this book—for persons active in very different cultural and political contexts over several millennia.

In this work the adviser is generally one whose advice has been proffered to the supreme leader of a nation. He may have provided counsel by either the spoken or the written word, or by both. I have not hesitated to include in my illustrations some persons who as first ministers have held official advisory posts, although in these cases they are generally advisers who have had close personal relations with the political leader and may, as in the case of Colonel House and Henry Kissinger, have held unofficial advisory posts before acquiring an official position. The political adviser may, then, be Aesop, Kautilya, Han Fei Tzu, Ibn Khaldun, Giraldus Cambrensis, Commynes, Machiavelli, Erasmus, Francis Bacon, Bismarck, Colonel House, Lord Cherwell, Harry Hopkins, John Ehrlichman, or Henry Kissinger, to name only a few. The appearance of, say, Shang Yang, Guicciardini, Richelieu, Metternich, and Theodore Sorenson in the same or neighboring sentences may be vertiginous, but even a casual examination of their writings and activities will confirm how enduring certain themes dealing with advice and the adviser have been through the ages and how readily the political advisers of the most diverse periods and nations would have understood, although not necessarily agreed with, each other.

Three additional principles have guided the selection of the illustrative materials I have used. First, I have drawn primarily on those who have had practical experience as advisers to, or as mentors of, the wielders of political power. This does not preclude attention to figures who themselves possessed supreme power. Louis XIV, James I, and Frederick the Great, for example, are of interest not only as rulers experienced in the choice of advisers and the reception of advice, but also as political advisers in their own right to their heirs. Although most of the persons whom the reader will encounter in the following pages were actors on the political scene and not just analysts of it, several were only marginal to the seats of power: Hobbes as tutor to the Prince of Wales and later as a frequenter of his court when he became Charles II, Aristotle as tutor for four years to Alexander the Great, and Gracián as a familiar of Philip III's dinner table. Plato, Jonathan Swift, Coleridge, and perhaps one or two others, are hardly political figures in the sense in which the term is generally used in this work, but our references to them will make clear the reasons for their brief appearances in the present company.

Second, the political figures discussed in this work are chosen not for their role in important historical developments but rather because of their contribution to the art of advising and decision making, and for their generalizations based on their own experience and their study of the past. As one proceeds through the centuries from the early Chinese, Indian, and Greek writers, through the early and later Middle Ages and the Renaissance, there is an almost inexhaustible amount of material from which to choose thoughtful reflections on the advisory process by participants in or close observers of the political process. But, as time wears on, and especially in the nineteenth and twentieth centuries, the most famous political memoir writers show a much greater interest in recording historical events than in pausing to reflect in a generalizing vein on their experiences in the manner that seemed almost second nature to a Han Fei Tzu, a Polybius, an Ibn Khaldun, a Commynes, a Machiavelli, or a Richelieu. Consequently, the memoirs and papers of men like Metternich, Bismarck, and Colonel House have a distinctly different character from those of earlier ages. On occasion they show in letters, diaries, and state papers brief flashes of a generalizing interest, but they did not have the sustained interest in analysis that characterized many early political figures. The persistent international wanderings of these early political advisers may have given them more of a comparative, generalizing interest.[1] Perhaps the development of social science disciplines disinclined the great nineteenth- and twentieth-century political figures from contributing in these areas. The decline of absolutism also reduced interest in the advisory relationship as such and gave prominence to the constitutional issues revolving around the powers of various officers of the realm and the councils and assemblies to which they belonged. In Britain much of this reflects the change from a king who was the prime consumer of advice and advisers to one who as a constitutional monarch is said to retain the right to *give* it.

Third, this work does not attempt to throw light on the substantive issues of domestic and foreign policy to which the political advisers with whom I deal contributed. These issues belong to the history of state and interstate behavior. The history of the adviser is not the same as the history of policy any more than the history of the doctor embraces the history of medicine, or the history of the lawyer the history of law. Of course, I have been concerned with some limited aspects of policy, but this is policy on the art of advising, the choice of advisers, and the utilization of advisers and advice. I have also been concerned with certain principles of policymaking—thus, for example, the role assigned to chance or unpredictability, the advantages and disadvantages of delaying action, the relative merits of explicit calculation and personal, intuitive judgment.

---

[1]On this point, see pages 76–83 below.

My essay begins with a review of the functions of the political adviser (Chapter 1), passes on to illustrate the sources and types of advice made available to the political leader (Chapter 2), then considers the advisers themselves and their selection (Chapter 3), the relations, often very delicate, between advisers and their principals and among advisers of the same principal (Chapter 4), and concludes with a discussion of several aspects of the decision-making process as viewed through the ages by different types of advisers (Chapter 5).

Citations in the footnotes have been abbreviated. Complete citations are available in the Bibliography.

1

"The Inseparable Conjunction of Counsel with Kings"

"Who hath directed the Spirit of the Lord,
or being his counsellor hath taught him?
With whom took he counsel, and who
instructed him . . . ?"[1]

For Isaiah, clearly, God alone can dispense with counsel.[2] Man is a different case, and few are the rulers who lay claim to the divine prerogative to act without counsel. The oldest literary and historical documents already show the counselor as much a part of the political structure as the king himself.[3] Ancient myths, Bacon wrote, show "the inseparable conjunction of counsel with kings."[4]

---

[1]Isaiah 40:13–14.

[2]Bacon, eager to stress the indispensability of the counselor, upheld a contrary opinion: "God himself is not without [counsel] but hath made it one of the great names of his blessed Son: *The Counsellor.*" Bacon, "Of Counsel," *Selected Writings,* p. 55.

[3]See, for example, *Gilgamesh* (pp. 64–65 below) and the *Shu Ching (Book of History),* ancient China's oldest historical document.

[4]Bacon, "Of Counsel," *Selected Writings,* p. 55.

This conjunction derives from various needs of the ruler and a corresponding variety of functions performed by the counselor—the counselor as a friend, educator, conscience, eyes and ears, executor, and adviser.

The Solitary Man

The persistence through the centuries of the image of the ruler as an isolated, lonely figure is a tribute to the dominance of certain common features of his position in the immense variety of historical circumstances in which this role has been played out. The ancient Chinese emperors and great feudal lords sometimes spoke of themselves as "the solitary man," "the lonely man," "the orphan," and begged their great officers and counselors to "take care of me, do not abandon me."[5] Writing to Henrietta Maria, Charles I complained: "There was never man so alone as I, and therefore very much to be excused for the committing of any error. . . ."[6] According to Shah Mohammed Reza Pahlevi of Iran, a king who is not accountable to anyone "is unavoidably doomed to loneliness."[7] General de Gaulle noted that it is the loneliness of the leader that produces "that vague sense of melancholy which hangs about the skirts of majesty."[8] The isolation of the ruler on his pinnacle of power, perhaps all the more isolated in some polities by virtue of the press about his person, has become a cliché of political biography and autobiography. But clichés are no less true for being such and American presidents as diverse in personality as Woodrow Wilson, Franklin D. Roosevelt, Harry S. Truman, John F. Kennedy, and Lyndon B. Johnson have been described or have spoken of themselves in much the same fashion, if somewhat less evocatively, as have, since ancient days, emperors and kings.[9]

Some abatement of the ruler's sense of loneliness and isolation is provided by an adviser who also serves as confidant and friend.

---

[5]*Shu King*, p. 263 and Couvreur, p. 158.
[6]H. Wragg, p. 45.
[7]Oriana Fallaci.
[8]de Gaulle, p. 66.
[9]Richard Nixon could also be described as "the solitary man," but he was, it seems, a self-isolating president.

Franklin D. Roosevelt's relations with Hopkins and Woodrow Wilson's with Colonel House are familiar examples. John F. Kennedy had in his brother, Robert Kennedy, not only an adviser and his attorney general, but also a close confidant.[10] Roosevelt commented that his successors would "learn what a lonely job this is, and . . . discover the need for somebody like Harry Hopkins who asks for nothing except to serve you."[11] In Great Britain the role played by Frederick Lindemann, later Lord Cherwell, as personal adviser to Churchill before, during, and after World War II (see pp. 71–72 and 89 below) paralleled an equally strong friendship.[12]

Friend, confidant, and adviser may, then, be one and the same person. But this does not always meet with approval. The function of "boon companion" to the ruler was sometimes, as in eleventh-century Persia, a particular office in the service of the ruler distinct from that of counselor or minister.[13] Guillaume Budé, author of a book of advice (c. 1518) dedicated to his master François I, recognized that it was important for the prince to have friends, but held that they must not be confused with the prince's counselors nor participate in government.[14] James VI warned his son: "Conferre not with hunters at your counsell, nor in your counsell affaires; nor dispatche not affaires at hunting or other games. . . . Be warre likewaies . . . in making your sporters your counsellers. . . ."[15] Commynes, too, and Bacon seem to assume a separation of these functions, although they do not discuss this explicitly.

An initial separation of the "boon companion" or favorite from the adviser or minister does not guarantee the former's exclusion from political influence. Indeed, the emotional ties that exist between the ruler and his favorite may precisely facilitate the latter's rise to power and his influence in matters of high policy. Richelieu, eager to distract Louis XIII and thereby to control him, promoted a relation between him and the young Cinq-Mars; the latter, however, became in consequence far too powerful to suit Richelieu's

[10]Sorenson, 1965, p. 267.

[11]Sherwood, p. 3. On Wilson and House see p. 89 and p. 110 below.

[12]Birkenhead, pp. 220, 224. See also C. P. Snow, pp. 64–65, and R. F. Harrod, p. 6.

[13]See Ibn Iskandar, chap. 38, "The Function of Boon Companionship."

[14]Budé, p. 65.

[15]James VI, *The Basilicon Doron*, vol. 1, p. 197.

purpose. Similarly, the favorites of James I—Carr, Somerset, and Buckingham—overshadowed the king's advisers and ministers. Lord Bute, tutor, companion, and confidant to the future George III, was raised to secretary of state by the king shortly after his accession to the throne and continued after his resignation to advise the king until the latter was finally forced to relinquish this source of counsel.[16] Louis XVIII was conscious that his high confidence in and reliance on his minister Élie Decazes was attributed by political observers to the friendship that the king felt for his young collaborator (see pp. 90–91 below) and not to the latter's great capacities. He complained of the lies and ignorance that led the European political world to confuse cause and effect.[17]

Rulers not infrequently found some alleviation for their sense of isolation in hunting,[18] jousting, feasting, and other distractions that sometimes complicated the work of advisers and ministers just as much as the king's close ties to his favorites and to his mistresses. And yet despite the opportunities open to the ruler to indulge his impulses and despite the eager ministrations of advisers, friends, and companions, his cry of loneliness—sometimes manifested in apprehension and paranoia—has persisted through the ages and suggests that for this royal complaint there is no sovereign cure.

The Conscience of the King

In the ancient Chinese tradition "the solitary man" was in greater need of moral instruction and admonition than the consolations of friendship. The advisers of the early emperors and kings had on their conscience the conscience of the king. Many of the wandering sages, especially of the Confucian type, who offered their services to the feudal lords, drew no sharp distinction between the provision of political wisdom and moral instruction. "How can he be said truly to be loyal who refrains from admonishing the object of his loyalty?"[19] The proliferation of officials and advisers did not

---

[16]On Lord Bute's relations with George III, see Ayling; Brooke.

[17]Roger Langeron, p. 273.

[18]Frederick the Great contemptuously charged that most kings and princes spend three-quarters of their life hunting and killing animals. *L'anti-Machiavel*, p. 254.

[19]*The Comprehensive Discussions in the White Tiger Hall*, vol. 2, p. 463.

eliminate this view of Chinese ministerial responsibilities. The political adviser, official, or sage who found his admonitions unheeded and therefore left his prince, or who withdrew totally from public life, or who suffered torture and death by virtue of his insistent remonstrances, long remained a major theme in Chinese writings.[20]

This theme is not absent in other societies and periods, but admonition of the king increasingly became the responsibility of specialized guardians of the moral order rather than of the king's ministers and advisers. The prophet (e.g., Jeremiah, Savonarola), the dervish, the hermit, the almoner, the priest, the confessor, and the court preacher take on in varying degrees the responsibility of reducing royalty to human proportions. "Choose for confessor," Louis IX, in his testament, told his son, "a right worthy man who knows how to teach thee what to do, and what not to do; and bear thyself in such sort that thy confessor and thy friends shall dare to reprove thee for thy misdoings."[21] "Surely in that most intimate confidence," wrote Erasmus, "[the royal confessor] could help the prince with loving and frank advice."[22]

The important political roles of many church figures in Europe up to the eighteenth century provided for some fusion of the roles of adviser and admonisher, but admonition at these high levels was more often inspired by power and policy conflicts than by the attempt to impose moral restraints and mitigate the cruelties and exactions of war and peace; these responded more to the efforts of the lesser clergy than to those in the highest places. Nonetheless, the histories of such churchmen as Thomas à Becket and such laymen as Sir Thomas More are not without elements that correspond to ancient Chinese themes.

---

[20]The Taoists, with their quietist tendencies and primary concern with the inward man, saw matters differently from the Confucians. One who was about to become preceptor to a vicious prince asked, "How is one to deal with a man of this sort?" The Taoist reply was: "The first thing you must do is not to improve him, but to improve yourself." There are two essentials: outward accommodation without affecting what is within; peace within that should not betray itself outside. "Be very careful not to meet a bad man's villainy by displaying to him what is best in you." The attempt to do good often suffers the fate of the man who so dearly loved his horse that when a fly settled on it, he struck at it. Taken by surprise, the horse plunged and tore its breast. Waley, pp. 108–110.

[21]Joinville, p. 321.

[22]Erasmus, *Education of a Christian Prince*, p. 196.

Admonition and moral instruction was a principal concern of the many "Mirrors of Kings," books of instruction for the prince, produced during antiquity, the Middle Ages, and the Renaissance. But these generalized exhortations to be and do good hardly had the potentiality for moral influence of either the morally concerned adviser or the aroused churchman. As Bacon dryly remarked, "Reading good books of morality is a little flat and dead. . . . Best is the admonition of a friend."[23]

The admonisher of the prince has long ceased to exist as an appealing official position. We note, then, with admiration that Montaigne, when asked what service he would have considered himself fit for had anyone thought to make use of him, chose precisely this function. "I should have had enough fidelity and judgment and frankness for that. It would be a nameless office—otherwise it would fail of its effect and its seemliness. . . ."[24]

With the advent of more democratic political institutions and the development of the pamphleteer, the periodical and daily press, the cartoonist, the press, radio, and TV commentator, there was no longer any dearth of critics and admonishers of those in high office, although hardly many of great moral stature and influence. John D. Ehrlichman, White House adviser and assistant to President Nixon, testified in a trial in which he was charged with the obstruction of justice, that "he [Nixon] said I had been or tried to be his conscience. I replied that I hadn't been as effective as I would have liked."[25] Evidently, in the modern world the conscience of the king, that is, of the political leader, is hardly a major preoccupation of anyone within his own entourage. As for the official representatives of the claims of religion and the moral order, they have nowadays largely been reduced to bestowing on ceremonial occasions a benediction rather than a reproof.

---

[23]Bacon, "Of Friendship," *Selected Writings*, p. 73.

[24]Montaigne, *Essays*, vol. 4, p. 308. Montaigne's choice of an office associated throughout history with torture and death reminds us of his advice that the education of the young should prepare them to bear prison and torture "which, according to the times, seize upon good men as well as bad." *Essays*, vol. 1, p. 206.

[25]*New York Times*, December 11, 1974.

"A Feeble Creature"

The political adviser does not always view even the most absolute ruler as an all-powerful and mighty figure. On the contrary, the ruler is often, as he was to the great fourteenth-century Arabic historian and political adviser Ibn Khaldun, "a feeble creature," who carries a heavy load and can only exercise political leadership with much assistance from others. *Wazir* (vizier), Ibn Khaldun pointed out, derives from words meaning "help" and "load," "as if the wazir were helping the person whom he supports to carry his burdens and charges."[26] For Kautilya, the tutor and first minister of Chandragupta, founder of the fourth-century B.C. Maurya dynasty, "sovereignty is possible only with assistance. A single wheel [of a chariot] can never move."[27] When, a few days before his inauguration, President-elect John F. Kennedy was presented with a list of 250 matters on which decisions were required, he remarked, "Now I know why Ike had Sherman Adams."[28]

Aristotle provided a whole succession of writers with a standard expression for the king's dependence on others. "It is . . . the practice of kings to make to themselves many eyes and ears and hands and feet."[29] The Persian officials who scrutinized the behavior of the satraps were called the Eyes and Ears of the King. Louis XIV, referring to the necessity of counsel, warned his grandson: "Our lofty position . . . separates us from our people to whom our ministers are closer, and are consequently able to see a thousand things of which we know nothing, but on which nevertheless we must make up our minds and take measures."[30] It was this dependence on others that led William Penn to moderate, with Quaker charitableness, criticism of the ruler. "It is certain [that] princes ought to have great allowances made them for faults in government, since they see by other people's eyes and hear by their ears."[31]

---

[26]Ibn Khaldun, *The Muqaddimah*, vol. 2, p. 6.
[27]Shamasastry, *Kautilya's Arthasastra*, p. 12.
[28]Sorenson, 1965, p. 238.
[29]Aristotle, *Politics*, bk. III, 1287^b.
[30]Louis XIV, p. 64.
[31]Penn, p. 54.

In sizable polities, advisers, friends, ministers, court attendants, and retainers provided too few eyes and ears, and especially in Asia elaborate spying systems developed very early for both domestic and foreign needs. Kautilya provides a striking account of the Indian case. Trained and organized by the institute of espionage, spies were densely posted throughout the realm. Living as students, housewives, monks, farmers, beggars, prostitutes, and in hundreds of other roles, they penetrated every cranny of the state, as well as engaging in foreign operations. Orphans, having no family loyalties, were often favored recruits for the espionage system. These spies, unknown to each other, reported to the institute of espionage that transmitted their information to higher levels after checking its validity. When information from three different sources coincided, it was held to be reliable, but if the three sources frequently differed, the spies were punished or dismissed. Counterespionage was also conducted.[32] In eleventh-century Persia an experienced prince warned his son: "During your reign as king do not neglect to inform yourself of the position of other kings in the world. The ideal at which you must aim is that no king shall be able to draw a breath without your being aware of it."[33]

The development of internal and external security and intelligence agencies, supported in the modern world by a specialized technology, led to new centers of information and power, often not subject to the control of the leader's chief political advisers or the political leader himself. Those immediately surrounding the ruler are sometimes able to filter and interpret information reaching him, but increasingly they have had to reckon with the competition of intelligence services that assert their right to act as the eyes and ears of the ruler. Even much less esoteric sources of information compete now with the personal representatives of the ruler. "I feel," said Prime Minister Trudeau in a television interview, "the whole concept of diplomacy today is a little bit outmoded. I believe much of it goes back to the early days of the telegraph when you needed a dispatch to know what was happening in a country, whereas now you can read it in a good newspaper."[34]

---

[32]Shamasastry, *Kautilya's Arthasastra*, pp. 17–22; see also Kangle, *The Kautilya Arthasastra*, pp. 21–27.
[33]Ibn Iskandar, p. 231.
[34]*The New York Times*, March 8, 1970.

The "feeble creature" is especially vulnerable and in need of assistance when he accedes to power at an early age with little or no experience of rule. The careful selection of tutors and advisers and the preparation of books written for young princes deal more especially with this problem (see pp. 37–41 and pp. 49–51). But even the experienced politician may find the sudden accession to power a period of stress in which counsel is urgently needed and the search for talent becomes a principal concern. The ten frantic weeks intervening between John F. Kennedy's election and his inauguration contrast with the more gradual preparation for high office of the prince, and perhaps, too, with the accession to power of a new British prime minister together with most of his "shadow cabinet."[35]

"A Drier and Purer Light"

The adviser as a friend and companion, as admonisher or keeper of the king's conscience, and as his eyes and ears, plays roles supplementary to what are generally viewed as his principal functions. He is, above all, a provider of judgment, wisdom, analytic and professional skills, with the ability to apply these talents to policy. This may involve a twofold task—*advice* on specific problems of policy, and *education* that seeks to improve the ruler's own judgment and knowledge and to generalize advice beyond the occasion of the moment. Secondly, the adviser may operate as a sounding board for, and perhaps critic of, the ruler's own ideas and plans. At times the adviser may primarily facilitate the leader's inner dialogue; the latter's interest in drawing others into discussion may be not so much to listen to their opinions as to hear what he himself thinks and says. Harry Hopkins "made it his job to provide a sounding board. . . . Roosevelt liked to think out loud, but his greatest difficulty was finding a listener who was both understanding and entirely trustworthy."[36] Bismarck, on the contrary, preferred solitary reflection.[37]

---

[35]See Schlesinger, 1965, chap. V, and Sorensen, 1965, chaps. IX and X. See also Truman, vol. 1, pp. 30, 48, and 482, and pts. I and II of Cronin and Greenberg. This volume provides much useful discussion of the present American presidential advisory system.

[36]Sherwood, p. 212.

[37]Holstein, vol. 1, p. 8.

Advisers and ministers stress the indispensable contribution that they make to the ruler and the state. For Motse, a Chinese political philosopher and military specialist of the fourth century B.C., one of the seven causes of worry to a state is "when the lord is over-confident of his own wisdom and holds no consultations."[38] Kautilya distinguished three kinds of strength of the ruler: wise counsel; wealth and military force; and personal enterprise.[39] The crucial determinant of a prince's effectiveness is, then, not his material strength but what goes on in his council. For Kautilya good decision making dominates material force.[40] Isocrates, author of one of the earliest books of advice to a royal personage, the young king of Cyprus, held that "a good counsellor is the most useful and the most princely of all possessions."[41] And Ibn Iskandar warned his favorite son that "he who relies entirely on his own judgment ever regrets it."[42]

For Commynes, adviser to both Charles, Duke of Burgundy, and Louis XI, "It is a cardinal fault in a prince to esteem his own opinion more than that of several others."[43] The wisest princes, wrote Bacon, need not think it any diminution of their greatness to rely on counsel. If issues "be not tossed upon the arguments of counsel, they will be tossed upon the waves of fortune. . . ."[44] Richelieu echoed Motse in writing that "The worst government is that which has no other guiding force than the will of an incompetent and presumptuous king who ignores his council."[45] The depth of Richelieu's conviction is suggested by the fact that this adviser and chief minister to Louis XIII had himself a trusted personal adviser and aide in Father Joseph.[46] Gracián put the importance of counsel

[38]Motse, p. 17. Motse's appreciation of the ruler's need for advice was accompanied by an equally acute appreciation of the adviser's need to avoid pure criticism. "Whoever criticizes others must have something to replace them. Criticism without [a positive] suggestion is like trying to stop flood with flood and put out fire with fire. It will surely be without worth." Ibid., pp. 87–88.

[39]*Sources of Indian Tradition*, p. 254.

[40]Much of military and political history as well as contemporary views on decision making tend to support Kautilya.

[41]Born, 1965, pp. 48–49.

[42]Ibn Iskandar, p. 33.

[43]Commynes, p. 396.

[44]Bacon, "Of Counsel," *Selected Writings*, p. 55.

[45]Richelieu, *Political Testament*, p. 57.

[46]On the relations of Père Joseph and Richelieu, see Fagniez and Huxley.

more bluntly than most, perhaps because he could hardly be supposed to aspire to high office under Philip III: "None is so perfect that he does not need at times the advice of others. He is an incorrigible ass who will never listen to anyone. . . . Sovereignty itself must learn to lean."[47]

The need for counsel is so apparent to the professional advisers that they are little disposed to bring arguments to bear in support of their claims. "Two heads are better than one" or the importance of long experience and knowledge may be alluded to or implied, but otherwise assertion is made to suffice. Occasionally special points lead to greater elaboration. Giraldus, a Welshman serving Henry II, attributed the errors of the English in their expeditions against the Welsh to their failure to use native advisers in place of those "ignorant of the manners and customs of the natives."[48] Commynes emphasized the ease with which princes are deceived when they rely only on their own judgment.[49] Bacon made special reference to the persistence of biases of thought and emotion which can only be countered by the "drier and purer light" of another man's disinterested counsel.[50]

Most writings on the adviser pictured him, implicitly, as a person who stands apart from action and casts his "drier and purer" light on troublesome questions faced by his principal. This certainly fits Patronio, the household counselor of Count Lucanor in Don Juan Manuel's *El Conde Lucanor*, a fourteenth-century "wisdom book."[51] It generally fits the adviser as admonisher and companion, and also many of the idealized portraits of the adviser in the Mirror of Kings literature (pp. 37–41 below). But in fact advisers rapidly get drawn into undertaking missions for their principal, and the distinction between the adviser and the executor or troubleshooter often disappears. The letters of the younger Pliny are primarily the letters of an administrator and troubleshooter, which is not surprising since Rome, unlike Greece, provided few writers who devoted themselves to general political analysis. Many of the advisers

---

[47]Gracián, pp. 86–87.
[48]Giraldus, *Itinerary Through Wales*, p. 130.
[49]Commynes, p. 98.
[50]Bacon, "On Friendship," *Selected Writings*, p. 73.
[51]Juan Manuel, *Count Lucanor*.

cited in the present work were also charged with missions that separated them at times from their masters. Commynes, Guicciardini, Machiavelli, Giraldus, and Botero are instances of this in earlier ages. In the American context, Colonel House and Harry Hopkins are obvious examples, but almost all White House staff advisers undertake a variety of tasks that go beyond a purely advisory function—speech writing, recruiting of talent, liaison, and others. This assignment of the adviser to numerous missions must necessarily affect his work as an adviser, if only because of the drain on his time. On the other hand, the contacts and experience accumulated in the course of these missions often provide an important basis for strengthening his advisory capabilities and his influence. Here again Colonel House and Harry Hopkins are prime examples of the increased prestige and authority of advisers following important missions abroad.

Today the vast body of government officials is too massive to be easily controlled by or to be made responsive to the political leader. He is led, therefore, to have recourse to a more compact and 'private' officialdom interposed between himself and the ministries and agencies of government. His chief advisers may become the organizers and leaders of these interposed organs, as was Henry Kissinger when he headed a staff of seventy-five persons in the National Security Council. This readily leads to rivalry between the new structure and other elements of government (see pp. 97–104).

The princes and rulers who are the recipients of so much wisdom are not quite so convinced of the indispensability of counsel as are the advisers themselves. Still, for the most part, when they discuss advisers or especially when they address themselves to their sons who are to succeed them, they repeat in large measure the good opinion of counsel and counselors that the latter express in their own writings. Louis IX, on his death bed, commanded his son to choose loyal men "and confer with them oft."[52] James VI and Louis XIV gave their successors similar advice. Charles V in his several secret advisory letters to his son provided information on the merits and limitations of different counselors and clearly encouraged his son to listen to them.[53]

---

[52]Joinville, p. 321.

[53]Laiglesia, pp. 69–76 and Armstrong, pp. 80–84.

For a self-confident ruler the inevitable constraints and frictions imposed by collaboration with advisers is likely to affect his acceptance of them. Louis XIV admonished his grandson to pay heed to advisers but nonetheless preferred to act as his own first minister.[54] The secretaries of state of Frederick the Great were often simply executors of his orders.[55] King James I "makes no haste to nominate any [secretary of state] but sayes he is prettelie skilled in the craft himself, and till he be thoroughly wearie will execute yt in person."[56]

Modern heads of state and of government can hardly dispense this easily with their ministers, but they show considerable variability in their readiness to seek and accept advice. Franklin D. Roosevelt "in 1932 was patient, amenable to advice. . . . As time went on and victories mounted, he grew impatient of advice. . . . He succumbed to the unlovely habit of telling, not asking."[57] It has been noted that the humility with which President Truman entered upon his responsibility after the death of Roosevelt gradually gave way to a self-confidence that made him less dependent on advisers and increasingly prone to sharp remarks about "experts." In his case, however, this seems to have been due not to the lordliness sometimes attributed to Roosevelt in his later years but rather to his possession of a simple and effective set of principles that guided his decisions and made the more convoluted calculations of the "experts" seem incompetence and confusion. Nonetheless, despite his reservations about experts, it was Truman who created the Council of Economic Advisers and the National Security Council within the Executive Office of the president.[58]

Reservations concerning the advisory function may derive not from any general disparagement or minimization of its value but from its inappropriateness in certain specific contexts, especially those where highly personal values and issues are involved. Metternich was, according to his testimony, unwilling to advise Francis II when Napoleon asked for the hand of the emperor's daughter.

---

[54]Louis XIV, p. 8.

[55]Benoist, pp. 80–81 and 87.

[56]Letter from John Chamberlain to Sir Dudley Carleton, English Ambassador at Venice, 11 June 1612, in Ashton, p. 76.

[57]Moley, p. 45.

[58]Truman, vol. 1, p. 493, and vol. 2, p. 58.

"There are cases in the life of states . . . in which calculation alone is not sufficient to lead to a decision. Your Majesty is Ruler and Father—to you alone it belongs to consider what is your duty."[59]

The almost universal attribution of presumptuousness to the person who systematically avoids advice hardly prepares us for considered statments of a dissenting opinion. But such a statement exists in one of the West's oldest writings, Hesiod's *Works and Days*: "That man is altogether best who considers all things himself . . .; and he, again, is good who listens to a good adviser; but whoever neither thinks for himself nor keeps in mind what another tells him, he is an unprofitable man."[60] This guarded view of asking advice as a second best measure was hardly widespread in ancient Greece. Homer's Agamemnon is constantly calling together his "captains and counselors," and when he asks the gods to help him to reduce Troy, it is not for great captains like Ajax that he asks: "If I only had ten such counselors [as Nestor]!" We find a similar thought in Ecclesiastes: "Wisdom strengtheneth the wise more than ten mighty men which are in the city."[61]

In the contemporary world a dissenting view on the necessity of advice has also been expressed by the Shah of Iran: "To get things done, one needs power, and to hold onto power one mustn't ask anyone's permission or advice. One mustn't discuss decisions with anyone."[62]

Preconditions

The rulers' need of or desire for advisers to provide the services discussed earlier—friendship, admonition, information, education, analyses and advice, special missions—would hardly have developed to the extent it did without the existence of certain persistent conditions that shaped the demand and supply of advisory personnel. The political advisers of the past and their princes were acutely aware of the various personal requirements of the ruler for

[59]Metternich, vol. 1., p. 119.

[60]Hesiod, lines 293–296.

[61]*The Iliad*, bk. 2, and Ecclesiastes 7:19.

[62]Oriana Fallaci.

advisers and ministers. They were, however, less conscious of the social and political circumstances that affected these requirements. There were nonetheless several conditions that the political advisers of past ages themselves recognized, although often only fleetingly.

It is evident that even in a miniscule state the single ruler requires the multiplication of himself through the eyes and ears of others, and this as we have seen (pp. 13–14 above) was very clearly understood. There was little discussion, however, of the effect of major variations in territorial and population size on the demand for administrative, military, technical, and political skills and of the consequent impetus to the development of classes of experts whose skill in one field often became a claim to influence and power in another.

The demand for political experts varies with political structure. In ancient China and India, in the European Middle Ages, in the Renaissance, and in the age of absolutism, most descriptions and discussions of the advisory process dealt with kingships where the need for additional eyes and ears for the king is particularly clear. In many democracies, however, sovereignty resides in an assembly, and the assembly already possesses in its own structure that multiplicity of eyes, ears, and judgments lacking to the solitary king. Greek discussion clearly reflects this difference. Plato had little esteem for the supposed merits of specialists in state affairs and held that politics could not be taught. A trained expertise was required in debates on, say, engineering tasks, but in political decisions every member of the assembly was entitled to express his views.[63] Nonetheless, both Greek practice and Aristotle's discussions recognized that political debate in the assembly required both advance preparations made by "preadvisers" who selected and formulated issues, and the contribution of political leaders whose wisdom and experience were often supplemented by gifts of rhetoric. In the Italian city-states—when their republican institutions were not reduced to impotence by tyrants—a multiplicity of councils made available to the government some participation of a substantial part of the citizenry, often on a rotating basis. Partly, of course, political assemblies and councils represent instruments for the distribution of power and the protection and promotion of a

[63]Plato, *Protagoras* (319).

variety of interests. But they are also consultative groups, and in this function they parallel that of advisers in a kingship or tyranny. In the Italian city-states the regularly constituted councils were sometimes viewed as not sufficiently knowledgeable, and special advisory or expert councils, the *pratiche,* were called together to deal with individual issues and decisions. These councils did not mean that a bureaucracy with a continuing staff could be dispensed with. It was as head of the second chancery for foreign affairs of Florence and not as an adviser of princes—except through his books—that Machiavelli exercised his political skills.

A third set of conditions affecting the demand and supply of advisers bears not on the size or political constitution of an individual polity, but on the number of such polities in its environment and the relations among them. The profession of adviser and the development of political skills as a fine art or practical science were most notable precisely where a multiplicity of small states lived in close proximity in a condition of continual rivalry, intrigue, and warfare. The development of a class of professional—often itinerant—political specialists, who advised a succession of princes and feudal lords and wrote important manuals on politics, government, and administration, was associated with these turbulent political conditions. China, in the long period of the Warring States (403–221 B.C.), produced, prior to its unification by the state of Ch'in, both a large class of political advisers and such notable works on the political art as *The Book of Lord Shang,* the writings of Han Fei Tzu, and the *Chan-kuo Ts'e*.[64] In India during the same period the rivalry of a number of small states[65] and Alexander's invasion of India in 325 B.C. provided similar experiences, similar personnel, and a similar concern to set down, as in the *Arthasastra*, a work attributed to Kautilya, the principles of statecraft necessary for state survival or state expansion. In North Africa in the thirteenth and fourteenth centuries, "innumerable kinglets, princelets, and feudal lords struggled for supremacy; towns changed masters with astonishing rapidity. . . ."[66] It was this background that produced Ibn Khaldun

---

[64]See pp. 40–41 below.

[65]Substantial population density and territorial expanse in ancient China and India gives the term "small state" a somewhat different meaning here than in Greece, or in fourteenth-century North Africa or in Renaissance Italy.

[66]Issawi, p. 3.

and other itinerant political specialists. The city-states of Italy in the fifteenth and sixteenth centuries reproduced similar conditions and a class of political specialists that included, among others, Machiavelli and Guicciardini. The small and rivalrous city-states of ancient Greece and their proximity to the great oriental despotisms are not without some responsibility for the development of Greek political skills and political literature. But their greater democratization and perhaps their greater bent for philosophical and scientific speculation seem to have hindered a fuller development of a literature on the practical arts of political manipulation and provided in its place political philosophy. The itinerant Sophists were specialists in rhetoric, that is, persuasion, and in some of the political arts, but were scarcely the equals of their counterparts in China.

The political advisers who in ancient China, India, North Africa, and Italy answered (or created) the demand for political expertise to deal with the dangers and difficulties provoked by multiple, quarreling states were aware of the bearing of these conditions on their own existence as a recognizable class of experts. Their long immersion in these conditions, however, probably prevented them from appreciating fully how special some of their own experiences were, although this was less true of the Italian experts in statecraft, living as they did on the periphery of the emerging national states and confronted by the power of France and Spain.

A fourth condition affecting the emergence of a class of political specialists is confidence that human will, effort, and intelligence count for something in human affairs, that an implacable destiny or fate does not rule over men. Political calculation and planning is predicated on such a conviction, but it cannot be taken for granted that this conviction always exists or is held deeply enough to sustain programs of political action. The expression of confidence in man, his accomplishments and abilities, in the superb chorus of Sophocles' *Antigone*—"wonders are many, and none is more wonderful than man," "man excellent in wit," "all the moods that mould a state, hath he taught himself,"—illustrates Greek conviction that man and his political institutions were equal to the challenges they faced.

The same sense of accomplishment and hope for the future informs Bacon's account of Salomon's House in the *New Atlantis:*

"The end of our foundation is the knowledge of causes, and secret motions of things; and the enlarging of the bounds of human empire, to the effecting of all things possible."[67] Bacon struck this note of optimism at a time when scientific accomplishments were still of a rudimentary character. But the developments of the next century and a half lent increasing reality to his vision.[68] Bacon's optimism did not prevent his prescient awareness that scientific accomplishments might create serious problems. The members of Salomon's House took oaths of secrecy with respect to some of their discoveries and sometimes withheld these from the state as well as from the public.

The sense of man's unlimited capacity for progress repeats itself from age to age, and Rousseau expresses some of the same amazement and admiration for man as did Sophocles. "It is a noble and beautiful spectacle to see man raising himself, so to speak, from nothing by his own exertions; dissipating, by the light of reason, all the thick clouds in which he was by nature enveloped; mounting above himself; soaring in thought even to the celestial regions; like the sun, encompassing with giant strides the vast extent of the universe. . . ."[69] Even what may seem to us so commonplace an accomplishment as the construction of the Crystal Palace, that "triumph of human thought and work" for the London Exposition of 1851, inspired an enormous sense of pride and unlimited perfectibility.

These convictions are, in some cultures, in a state of constant struggle with a profound sense of fatalism. Although both Greek and ancient Chinese society had pronounced fatalistic strains, these never dominated politics and political leadership. In Greece, knowledge and mind were esteemed as instruments of a contemplative life but this did not signify that political planning and political ends were beyond human control or rational pursuit. And still less was Rome disposed to isolate knowledge and reason from the interests of action and practical life. Cicero, while treading delicately for fear he might not seem sufficiently appreciative of

---

[67]Bacon, "New Atlantis," *Selected Writings*, p. 574.

[68]This did not prevent more cynical minds from observing, as Swift did in his Academy of Lagado, that both scientists and political philosophers could exploit man's optimism for their own self-advancement.

[69]Rousseau, p. 130.

philosophic wisdom, nonetheless affirmed that the establishment of a stable state "requires by far the highest intellectual powers that nature can produce."[70]

Although Taoism in China provided a strong strain of support for quietism and inaction in both private and public life, the political exigencies and opportunities of the period of the Warring States imposed their own claims on man's confidence in and capacity for political action. Legalist or realist writers like Lord Shang, Li Ssu, and Han Fei Tzu were hardly put off by the "talkers" who either on moral, quietistic, or other grounds preached inaction and withdrawal from political life. Motse attributed governmental difficulties in his lifetime to the effect of fatalism. "But from antiquity to the present, since the beginning of man, has anyone . . . heard the sound of fate or seen such a thing as fate? Of course, no one has."[71] Motse refers to the famous secretaries and ministers of the past whose "fame . . . has come down to the present day. The whole world remarks: 'This is the result of endeavor.' And it will never say: 'I see fate here.'"[72] He quotes to similar effect what is apparently a lost passage of the *Shu Ching* or *Book of History*, ancient China's oldest document: "Assuredly there is no fate in Heaven. Let us two not teach false doctrines. One's destiny does not come from Heaven, but is shaped by one's self."[73] From very early days Chinese thought tended to be political thought and aimed at the good society, whereas Indian thought stressed otherworldly goals.[74]

Islam also introduced an outlook that was potentially inimical to political planning and calculation. The confidence in political control and rational calculation implied by the importance Lord Shang attributed to "the thirteen figures" or administrative statistics (see pp. 136–137 below) contrasts strikingly with a Moslem response to the statistical inquiry of a Westerner:

> The thing which you ask of me is both difficult and useless. Although I have passed all my days in this place, I have neither counted the houses nor inquired into the number of inhabitants; and as to what one

[70]Cicero, *The Republic*, p. 191.
[71]Motse, p. 190
[72]Ibid., p. 191.
[73]Ibid., pp. 192–193.
[74]Arthur Wright, p. 34.

> person loads on his mule and another stores away in the bottom of his ship, that is no business of mine. . . . Listen, oh my son! There is no wisdom equal to the belief in God! He created the world and shall we liken ourselves to Him seeking to penetrate into the mysteries of His creation? Shall we say, behold! this star spinneth around that star, and this other star with a tail goeth and cometh in so many years? Let it go! He from whose hand it came will guide it and direct it. . . . Thou art learned in the things I care not for, and as for that which thou hast seen, I spit upon it. . . . Thy meek in spirit, Imaum Ali Zadi.[75]

In the more liberal atmosphere of Persia, Islam took more pride in human capabilities: "With the exception of him [God] all has become knowable."[76]

In the West, the Church sought to impose on the political process a regard for God's will and the necessity of divine grace and collaboration, but it was hardly opposed to an activist, rational outlook among political leaders. God's possible intervention was not infrequently taken into account in making political and military decisions, but this certainly did not mean that man's deliberations and planning were futile. Similarly the considerable role attributed during the Renaissance to chance or *Fortuna* meant that these forces had to be reckoned with, not that reckoning was useless or that man was a mere plaything of blind forces.

We have reviewed here only those conditions that the early advisers themselves noted as fostering in one degree or another a class of political experts. Clearly there are additional circumstances that, particularly in the modern world, multiplied enormously the importance of advisory services, more especially the great growth in scientific, technical, and engineering knowledge and skills, and in the economic, social, and military problems to which they were applicable. The early advisers to the ruler were primarily aware of the impact of technical developments on their profession in the case of military technology and leadership. So little was military expertise isolated from general political leadership that Motse could include in his treatise chapters on ethics, political organization, and military tactics. Similarly, Lord Shang was both political leader and

---

[75] I regret that I have lost the reference for this passage which has been in my files for a number of years.

[76] Ibn Iskandar, p. 7.

general, and almost two thousand years later Machiavelli wrote both on statecraft and warfare, and served Florence in both capacities. Kingship, throughout much of the history of this institution, called for skills in military as well as political leadership.

The early writers on statecraft could hardly have anticipated the effect of the more peaceful technical arts and sciences on the demand for advisory services. In the ancient empires enormous technical undertakings such as the irrigation systems of China, the walls and battlements, the temples, and the monuments of antiquity produced a special class of technical personnel, but they rarely achieved power in the political sphere as did those who were skilled in religious functions or in administrative or military arts. It remained for the technical accomplishments and problems of the nineteenth and twentieth centuries to impose on government leaders requirements that greatly increased the types and numbers of experts and advisers and produced a whole series of organizational devices to train, mobilize, and exploit their services.

2

Forms of Advice

'The adviser' evokes the image of one placed close to the ruler, of one who, for the most part, communicates his advice orally. When, however, we review the various means by which the ruler has, over the centuries, sought or received aid in his policy deliberations, this image is rapidly effaced by a great many others—the ruler searching in dreams, portents, divinations, and oracles for clues to the safety of himself and his realm; the ruler seeking for guidance in proverbs and fables, in wisdom books and in manuals of princely rule written to his intention; the ruler and his advisers sifting the historian's treasures for lessons in the art of statecraft; the young prince absorbing from a tutor lessons intended to serve him in the days of his majority; the king seated before his council of state in formal session; the modern ruler poring over a succession of reports, the filtered and abridged products of a voluminous outpouring of commissions, committees, task forces, research and policy institutes, that is, of an immense structure of institutionalized advisory services. Nor do these images by any means exhaust those that the history of the adviser can provide.

The World Above

The primal source of advice is the gods, who when properly approached and understood provide warnings, predictions, and counsel. They may even provide at birth, for each person, a tutelary or guardian angel who guides that person's actions, a belief shared by Pythagoras, Plato, and the early Roman church.[1] It was the Emperor Constantius' conviction that his tutelary angel's desertion of him presaged his death.[2] A thousand years later, Machiavelli was not entirely disposed to discard this belief.

An equally intimate source of advice is the dream, which both among preliterate peoples and in highly developed cultures is often viewed as a message from the gods. "If there be a prophet among you, I, the Lord, will make myself known unto him in a vision, and will speak unto him in a dream."[3] "For God speaketh once, yea twice, yet man perceiveth it not. In a dream, in a vision of the night, when deep sleep falleth upon men, in slumberings upon the bed; then he openeth the ears of men, and sealeth their instruction. . . ."[4] Unlike the guardian angel, the dream required interpretation and interpreters, and this gave rise to a class of counselors skilled in this craft. "Dream," says the Talmud in a striking image, "is the unripe fruit of prophesy."[5] Both Joseph's ascendance as counselor over Pharaoh and Daniel's over Nebuchadnezzar stemmed from their successful interpretations of the dreams of these great kings.[6]

A sense of close contact with the world above still occurs in the contemporary world. The inevitable loneliness stemming from the exercise of absolute power has been mitigated for the Shah of Iran because "I'm not entirely alone. . . . A force others can't perceive accompanies me. . . . I receive messages. I have lived with God beside me since I was five years old," a presence manifested

---

[1]Browne, *Religio Medici*, p. 356

[2]Marcellinus, *Julian the Apostate*, bk. 17.

[3]Numbers 12:6.

[4]Job 33:14–16.

[5]Maimonides, chap. 36.

[6]Genesis 41 and Daniel 2.

through visions, and by dreams which enable the Shah to see "what would happen within two or three months."[7]

The god also speaks through oracles, but speaks so obliquely that here, too, the oracle gives rise to an art of interpretation. "The god of the Delphic oracle," said Heraclitus, "does not speak, he does not dissemble: he points the way."[8] The Delphic oracle, where Apollo's voice was to be heard, was only one of several Greek centers where the gods spoke to man. Zeus had his own oracles at Dodona and Olympia.

Heaven and the gods spoke more plainly—generally of their displeasure and their demand for moral reform—in portents and prodigies. Floods, earthquakes, eclipses, droughts, plagues, comets, and the birth of monsters were messages not easily ignored. But many far lesser events seemed equally portentous. Just after Vitellius had been saluted by his troops in Germany as emperor, a stove set fire to the dining room of his headquarters. This unlucky portent caused concern to the troops, but Vitellius with quickness of mind cried out, "Courage, my men! Light is given us."[9]

The preoccupation with portents common to the Greeks, Romans, and Chinese was of great political importance. The displeasure and warnings of Heaven or the gods were generally presumed to be directed at the political authorities. In China this permitted the bureaucracy and opponents of the regime to record and report a large number of portents in order to bring the emperor to account.

It would have been awkward from a decision-making standpoint had no means existed for determining, upon demand, the proper resolution of an issue or the future context in which policy was to be exercised. In Greece the oracles might be consulted, but this often involved difficult travel, and without the certainty that the oracle would respond. Divination provided a more rapid access to the will of the gods. Both in China and Rome political stability and the well-being of the state depended on a delicate balance between heaven and earth. In Rome the decisions of both private and public life required the preservation of a correct relation with the gods,

---

[7]Oriana Fallaci.

[8]*Les penseurs grecs avant Socrate,* p. 79.

[9]Suetonius, *Vitellius.*

and such relations were made manifest by favorable auspices, favorable as interpreted by competent authority, that is, by a Roman magistrate. "Romulus," pointed out Cicero, "placed chief dependence upon the auspices—a procedure which continues even at the present day to contribute greatly to the safety of the state."[10] And contributed, too, to the importance of the augur and the haruspex skilled in reading the entrails of beasts, the flight of eagles, and the fall of stars.

In ancient China, divination by cracks in heated tortoise shells and by the stalks of a plant, the milfoil, were of great political importance. When, after the unification of China, the Burning of the Books occurred (213 B.C.), the *I Ching*, a book of divination, was one of the few to be spared. The *I Ching*, popularized in the West by Carl Jung, is, after twenty-five hundred years, still in use in private—one hopes not in public—life.

Astrology provided further indications concerning the moments propitious for decisions and actions. The Emperor Vespasian had such confidence in his own horoscope and those of his family that he left unharmed a potential rival for the throne although warned that this man had a horoscope indicating imperial rule.[11] Astrology has continued to be a source of political advice. Hitler is only one of the more famous modern rulers who listened to astrologically based advice. President María Estela Martínez de Perón of Argentina was supported in her decisions by adviser-astrologer José López Rega, her minister of social welfare.[12] President Lon Nol of Cambodia, a superstitious man, jailed fifty-five of Cambodia's astrologers in April 1973 for prophesying that he would be overthrown within a month.[13]

The claims of empiricism and self-reliance were not so limited as to leave the beliefs reviewed above unchallenged. The prominence given to some of the more bizarre manifestations of human dependence on the unseen world sometimes risks neglect of those who viewed these forms of behavior as childish or foolish. By Plutarch's time (first century A.D.), the business of the Greek oracles

---

[10]Cicero, *Commonwealth*, p. 161.

[11]Suetonius, *Vespasian*.

[12]The Economist, *Foreign Report* (London), September 11, 1974, p. 4.

[13]*The Economist*, April 7, 1973, p. 32.

had declined sharply. Delphi formerly had had two priestesses on duty with a third in reserve. In Plutarch's day, there was only one priestess and she more than sufficed.[14] Cicero, although himself an augur, held that dream interpretation and divination were superstitions.[15] Nonetheless, he believed that they promoted observance of the law and controlled the excesses of democracy. Referring to astrologers, Seneca asked: "What is to be gained from this sort of knowledge? Am I supposed to feel anxious when Saturn and Mars are in opposition. . . ."[16]

In China, too, a strong strain of secular thought challenged conventional beliefs. Hsüntze affirmed: "If people pray for rain and get rain, why is that? I answer: . . . If people do not pray for rain, it will nevertheless rain. . . . When they decide an important affair only after divination—this is not because they think in this way they will get what they seek. . . ."[17] Han Fei Tzu warned the ruler: "If the ruler believes . . . in divination and lot-casting . . . then ruin is possible. . . . [If] his mind is paralysed by the signs of future events . . . then ruin is possible."[18] He spoke more sharply in another passage: "Tortoise shells, bamboo slips, devils, and deities are not qualified to guarantee victory; nor are the directions of the stars . . . qualified to decide the outcome of war. . . . To believe in them is more stupid than anything else."[19] The *Chan-kuo Ts'e* regarded divination and diviners as useful tools for political intrigue.[20] Much later, in the Sung dynasty, Wang An Shih slyly asked civil service candidates the following question. After pointing out that floods and other disasters also occurred during the reign of good emperors, he asked, "What crimes had these rulers committed . . .? I suppose these words need very deep thought and

---

[14]Plutarch, "The Obsolescence of Oracles," *Moralia*, vol. V, pp. 351–501.

[15]"If the gods send us these unintelligble and inexplicable dream-messages they are acting as Carthaginians and Spaniards would if they were to address our Senate in their own vernacular without the aid of an interpreter. . . . Surely the gods ought to want us to understand the advice they give us for our good." Cicero, *On Divination*, p. 519

[16]Seneca, p. 155.

[17]Hsüntze, pp. 181–182.

[18]Han Fei Tzu, vol. 1, pp. 134 and 137.

[19]Ibid., vol. 1, p. 158.

[20]Crump, 1964, p. 11. See also pp. 40–41 below.

cannot be explained in any superficial way. Will you give me your ideas on this subject?"[21]

Solicitation of the world above in decision making was still sufficiently frequent in the sixteenth century to move Guicciardini to condemn astrology in the strongest language.[22] A century later, James VI warned his son: "Consult therfore with no Necromancier. . . ."[23]

There were, to be sure, positions between the firmly convinced believer in summoning the gods to his assistance and those who regarded this with total disdain. In China the *Comprehensive Discussions in the White Tiger Hall* (A.D. 79) suggested that in seeking advice the king should first consult with his ministers, then with the common people, and only then the tortoise shell and milfoil. "Why must the king first consult with his Ministers? Because first he should exhaust man's resources."[24] Consulting the tortoise shell and milfoil, on the other hand, indicates an avoidance of willfulness. Epictetus, too, wanted men to resort to the counsel of the gods only when their own resources of reason no longer sufficed.[25]

Wisdom and Wisdom Books

Well before a written literature was at their disposal, rulers possessed a source of guidance in the oral poets, and in proverbs and fables, the repositories of communal wisdom. Although these sources of counsel continued to have a large popular component, they developed forms that were more especially suited to those who exercised power. The Anglo-Saxon *scop* and the French *trouvère,* poets who exercised a public function, addressed themselves to audiences in the halls of lords and princes. Proverbs, "the storehouses of Minerva," developed several strains, some of popular origin, simple and of little subtlety, and others, the adages, providing advice based on the sayings of the poets and of learned

[21]Wang An Shih, vol. I, p. 344.
[22]Guicciardini, *Maxims*, p. 94.
[23]James VI, *Basilicon Doron*, vol. 1, p. 99.
[24]*Comprehensive Discussions in the White Tiger Hall*, vol. 2, p. 523.
[25]Epictetus, vol. 2, p. 228.

and wise men, and appealing more especially to those of higher social rank. The wisdom stored in these various types of sayings was still held, during the Renaissance, to be equally applicable to the decisions of private and public life. When Piero de' Medici announced that he was about to return to Florence, a Florentine council felt the threat could be disregarded, citing as a persuasive premise to this judgment the proverb "Barking dogs don't bite."[26]

Proverbs, aphorisms, and maxims did not remain purely popular oral or written recapitulations of sayings derived from oral tradition. They became a medium for recording more sophisticated observations, precepts, counsels, and reproofs for the benefit of those in the highest ranks of society, although of course the exclusiveness of the audience declined with the growth of literacy and wealth. Their content reflects the high degree of attention to royal and political behavior that one might have anticipated from the close relations many of the most famous writers of aphorisms and maxims such as La Rochefoucauld, Gracián, and Guicciardini had to the thrones and courts of their time.

Today we tend to approach this literature of maxims and aphorisms as entertaining reading for idle moments, but in the ages when written guidance to the problems of public and private policy was scarce, they received far more deliberate and concentrated attention. Guicciardini's maxims, the distillation of a lifetime of experience in politics, diplomacy, and business, were not intended for publication but were left—not as a memento but as a valuable legacy—for his family. It is one thing to read these and other maxims as a testimony to man's perspicacity, wit, and moral outlook. It is another matter to read them while carefully pondering their significance for one's own past, present, and future actions. Read in this spirit, they take on some of the meaning that they had in an earlier age.

The fable, by which is almost always meant the animal fable, became, more than the proverb, a form of instruction for the literate and the powerful, and more explicitly than the proverb dealt with

---

[26]Felix Gilbert, p. 38. The political wisdom borrowed from the lore of private life was well repaid when works especially written to guide the ruler became guides to private action as well. Machiavelli's *Prince* is the great instance of this, and Gabriel Harvey in Elizabethan England was only one of many who sought to make Machiavelli's teachings applicable to the pursuit of private objectives.

matters relevant to the art of ruling. Animal fables antedate by many years—and probably centuries—their first written collections and in their oral form, no doubt, had a broader audience. When they first emerge in written versions, they are already identified with the art of ruling. The first fable of an Aesopic type in Greek literature appears in one of Greece's oldest works, the *Works and Days* of Hesiod, who begins an animal fable with the words, "And now I will tell a fable for princes. . . ."[27] Aristotle, who preserved several fables that he attributed to Aesop, believed fables to be particularly useful in the political life of democracies: "Fables are suitable for addresses to popular assemblies; and they have one advantage—they are comparatively easy to invent, whereas it is hard to find parallels among actual past events."[28] Han Fei Tzu, on the other hand, viewed the use of the fable and other "homely counsels" in addressing the king as "unrefined."[29]

In India the fables of *The Panchatantra,* like those of Aesop in the Mediterranean world, were not intended as works of amusement. They were in the Indian phrase, *niti-shastra,* texts of the wise conduct of life.[30] We are told in the first pages of *The Panchatantra* that it was written by one of the king's counselors who undertook at the king's request to transform his three sons, "supreme blockheads," into three intelligent young men. The stories of *The Panchatantra,* especially Book III, reflect their intended application to political and military affairs.[31] Aesop, whose more or less mythical

---

[27]Hesiod, *Works and Days,* line 201. Like so many fables dealing with the art of rule, the fable of the Hawk and the Nightingale recorded by Hesiod, deals with the cruel realities of the powerful and the weak. The hawk, gripping the nightingale fast in his talons, speaks disdainfully: "Miserable thing, why do you cry out? One far stronger than you now holds you fast, and you must go wherever I take you. . . ." The hawk, the spokesman of power, ends with the dictum: "He is a fool who tries to withstand the stronger. . . ."

[28]Aristotle, *Rhetoric,* bk. II, 1394[a].

[29]Waley, p. 241.

[30]The principal text of *The Panchatantra* dates only from about 200 B.C., but the fables already existed in ancient times. The twelfth-century European animal epic of Reynard the Fox differs from the short Greek and Indian animal fables. *Reynard* was intended to entertain its audience by satirizing the nobility and the rich, and not to instruct in politics and the art of living.

[31]Book III of *The Panchatantra* should be compared with the Greek *Battle of the Frogs and Mice,* popularly ascribed to Homer. See Hesiod, *The Homeric Hymns and Homerica,* pp. 543–563.

biography is, significantly, that of a political adviser of international repute, apparently derived many of his animal fables from the same early sources used by the compilers of *The Panchatantra*. These, and the writings of other fabulists, were employed as serious prescriptions for behavior well into the Renaissance. Erasmus recommended the reading of Aesop in the education of the prince.[32] Already in Bacon, however, one finds the observation that the fable more appropriately provided lessons of wisdom in earlier ages when historical examples either did not exist or were not so accessible. "Now that the times abound with history," Bacon preferred, with Machiavelli, that examples be chosen from historical narratives.[33]

By the nineteenth century, Aesop had begun to lose much of his didactic significance and had become an entertainment and a children's book. But for Abraham Lincoln, Aesop was still that "great fabulist and philosopher," and in a campaign circular to the people of Illinois, he illustrated his theme that in union is strength by Aesop's fable of the bundle of sticks.[34] Even today, in France, there is no more acceptable way to define a situation or to reinforce an argument than to make the appropriate citation from La Fontaine.

Animal fables provided a device for discussing human—often royal—behavior without the indiscretion or indelicacy that might have resulted from the use in these stories of human actors. Under some circumstances, La Fontaine said, a man must be silent or "strike from afar." Still, the animal masks imposed—despite the very human traits attributed to these animals—some limitations on the nature and persuasiveness of the political lessons that the fable could convey. The Aesopian fable took a more 'human' direction in Don Juan Manuel's *El Conde Lucanor* (see p. 17 above). This halfway house between the animal fabulist and the manuals of statecraft converted the animal characters of Aesop into human and, very occasionally, historical characters.

The fictional setting for conveying important political lessons—and political propaganda—attained an elaborate development in

---

[32]Erasmus, *Education of a Christian Prince*, p. 146.

[33]Bacon, "Advancement of Learning," *Selected Writings*, p. 353. Still, Bacon, in his *Wisdom of the Ancients*, discerned in Greek mythological stories important truths concerning human and political relations, and in this anticipated writers like Vico and Jung. See Bacon, *Essays* (1883 ed.), pp. 271–371.

[34]Abraham Lincoln, vol. I, p. 315.

utopian literature, that is, literature that dealt with fictional ideal polities. Utopian literature, with its implied comparisons with real polities, was an instrument of admonition to rulers, but its intended audience was much broader. Like the fable, it provided an opportunity to advance political positions that might have been dangerous or embarrassing in a direct political commentary.

The use of a utopian tale to add a totally different dimension to one's political influence is exemplified in modern American history by Colonel House, who, in addition to his extraordinary influence over President Wilson between 1911 and 1918, wrote in 1911 and published anonymously in 1912, a novel, *Philip Dru: Administrator*. This is the story of a West Point graduate who leads the rebels against the plutocracy and the corrupt political class in a new American civil war, establishes himself as dictator for seven years, imposes a benevolent new legal, political, and social order on the country, and then voluntarily retires to permit a genuine democracy to work by itself. The quasi-socialist tenor of Philip Dru's sentiments, the uncompromising attack on the exploitative and corrupt behavior of the rich and of the political class, the demand, among others, for a thorough equality of the sexes not even achieved in the United States of today, are astonishing, even under the cloak of anonymity, in the man who was at the time President Wilson's closest adviser. The anonymous publication by Colonel House of his novel illustrates a principle of political action explained by his hero Philip Dru: "If we would convince and convert, we must veil our thoughts and curb our enthusiasm, so that those we would influence will think us reasonable."[35]

The Mirrors of Kings: Manuals of Statecraft

The central role of the prince or king in most western and eastern political structures from antiquity until the eighteenth century and the enormous consequences for their societies of their intelligence, knowledge, skills, ambitions, characters, and moral qualities made

[35][House], *Philip Dru: Administrator*, p. 64. The criticisms of the U.S. political, economic, and social scene in this novel are all the more striking since the novel is not set in some distant future but is virtually contemporaneous (1920) with its year of publication (1912). It is worth noting that in international affairs Philip Dru showed a far less progressive spirit than in his domestic program.

it almost inevitable that great attention would be paid to the possibility of influencing their development and behavior. This concern produced a large body of advisory literature far more systematic and deliberate than the proverbs, maxims, fables, and wisdom books considered above. These works were given the name "mirrors of kings" or "mirrors of princes" (*speculum principis*). In the dedicatory letter to Louis VIII in the *Gesta Philippi Augusti* we read: "You will always have before your eyes like a mirror the commendable acts of such a prince, as an example of virtue."[36]

These manuals intended to educate and assist the ruler had several sources. In medieval Europe a number of them were written by churchmen like Thomas Aquinas, Giraldus Cambrensis, and John of Salisbury. Particularly interested in moral and religious admonition, they tended toward the description of the ideal prince, but included some advice on problems of political and administrative import. A second source were manuals written by experienced political advisers or ministers such as Machiavelli, Botero, and Richelieu who sought to advance their fame and careers and to educate the ruler in order to promote their domestic and foreign policies. These manuals tended to deal more largely with political strategems and the rules of good statecraft. A third source was the rulers themselves who wrote manuals primarily—at least ostensibly so—for the benefit of their sons whose youth and inexperience required this testamentary advice.[37]

Between the twelfth and seventeenth centuries in Western Europe more than 100 Mirrors of Kings were written.[38] Clearly these works did not merely represent a fashionable literary genre. They

---

[36]Cited in Spiegel, p. 319.

[37]Although the motive to provide guidance to their sons was no doubt sincere, some royal books written for royal offspring were also motivated by the king's desire to justify his actions before history and to acquire the reputation of a learned man. These considerations probably applied to Louis XIV's letters to his heirs and to James VI's *Basilicon Doron,* although James claimed that his book had not originally been intended for publication.

[38]Born, 1928b, pp. 540–543, provides a far from complete list of 111 Mirrors of Princes written between 1159 (John of Salisbury) and 1700. These works are distributed by country as follows: England 11, France 25, Italy 31, Germany 22, Spain and Portugal 9, all others 13. The sixteenth century was particularly prolific. Allan H. Gilbert estimates that between A.D. 800 and 1700 some 1,000 books of advice to princes were written if one includes books in which a distinguishable part is dedicated to this subject. Allan H. Gilbert, 1938, p. 4.

were indeed read, studied, and taken very seriously. Many were written for a particular prince or ruler, but often reached a broader audience, particularly the children of the nobility or the princes of other ruling families. Mothers of princes and of other highborn children were not too proud to have books intended for other royal children translated for the use of their own children. Erasmus wrote his *Education of a Christian Prince* for Prince Charles, the future Charles V, but it went through eighteen editions and several translations in Erasmus' lifetime. Catherine de Médicis had a French paraphrase made for her sons. Count Frederick II of Bavaria required Prince Philip to read this work or a similar Mirror of Kings for three hours each day. Louis XI paid 30 gold *écus* to get an early Mirror of Kings translated into French for himself. James VI of Scotland (James I of England and Scotland) had a collection of Mirrors of Kings in his library. The one he wrote for his own son was seized upon by the ambassadors of Continental states and sent back to their governments where it was translated and searched for clues to the principles of statecraft and future policies of the new English king.[39]

The Mirrors of Kings are of interest here not only because they were an important type of counsel and source of advice for the ruler, but also because, as noted earlier, one of the most consistent pieces of advice given in them is that kings must have wise counselors and consult with them regularly. Born summarizes the content of the thirteenth- and fourteenth-century Mirrors of Kings as follows: "The perfect prince of the thirteenth and fourteenth centuries must be wise, self-restrained, just; devoted to the welfare of his people; a pattern in virtues for his subjects; interested in economic developments, an educational program, and the true religion of God; surrounded by efficient ministers and able advisers; opposed to aggressive war; and, in the realization that even he is subject to law, and through the mutual need of the prince and his subjects, zealous for the attainment of peace and unity."[40]

When we pass to the sixteenth and seventeenth centuries, to writers like Machiavelli and Richelieu, moral and religious concerns

---

[39]For the history of Western Mirrors of Kings, see Born, 1928a, 1928b, and 1965; Allan H. Gilbert, 1938; and James VI, *Basilicon Doron*, vol. II.
[40]Born, 1928a, p. 504.

decline and the Mirrors of Kings become what one can more appropriately call manuals of statecraft.

The Mirror of Kings was not a Christian and European monopoly. Comparable works were written in antiquity by both the Greeks and the Romans, although the Greek contribution is the larger and more outstanding. Isocrates' (436–338 B.C.) *To Nicocles* and Xenophon's (430–354 B.C.) *Cyropaedia* or *Education of Cyrus* were among those best known to European writers, if we exclude Plato's and Aristotle's political writings as belonging to a quite different genre. The city-states of Greece, and Roman republicanism, did not provide political environments suitable for the fuller development of a Mirror of Kings literature, and it is understandable that Xenophon found in an oriental despotism the setting for his portrait of the ideal education of the young ruler.

In the ancient world the Chinese and the Indians produced well-developed manuals of statecraft for rulers that were not rivaled in Europe until Machiavelli. In China, Lord Shang and Han Fei Tzu were the most eminent representatives of treatises marked by a certain realism, analytic hardheadedness, and perhaps cynicism, which sets them off from Chinese political writers in the Confucian and Taoist traditions whose moralistic and humanist writings were associated with a more aphoristic and anecdotal treatment of political problems.[41] Motse represented a systematizing tendency combined with a deep ethical concern.

The *Chan-kuo Ts'e*, a pre-Han document assembled from fragments by a first century A.D. Han palace librarian, is a reversion to the anecdotal format for providing political wisdom. This work is a series of anecdotes alleged to be historical but in fact invented in many instances for the purpose of political instruction. Its cynical schemes for achieving political and military mastery together with its relative scarcity gave it the reputation of a sinister and secret book, a knowledge of which virtually guaranteed political victory to those who had access to it.[42] A great admirer of this work was Yüan Yüeh (A.D. 370). "Yüan Yüeh was a skillful speaker, very

---

[41]An additional interest attaches to Lord Shang and Han Fei Tzu today. They are the preferred ancient writers of the government of the Chinese People's Republic. Confucius, on the other hand, has been subjected to a sustained attack.

[42]On the history of the *Chan-kuo Ts'e*, see Crump, 1970.

accomplished at *ch'ang-tuan* persuasions, and highly intelligent as well. . . . He returned to the capital and the only gift he offered anyone was a copy of the *Chan-kuo Ts'e*. He would say to them, 'When I was young I used to read the *Analects, Lao-tzu*, and even *Chuang-tzu* and the *Book of Changes*, but these works are all just so many headaches. What possible benefits can they yield? The one important thing in the world is *Chan-kuo Ts'e*!'" Presumably the book had some defect, since Yüan Yüeh had almost the whole empire in his grasp when he was suddenly executed by the king.[43]

The Indian counterpart to the treatises of Lord Shang and Han Fei Tzu is the previously dicussed *Arthasastra* of the Brahman Kautilya. This work supplanted an earlier aphoristic literature that had served as a guide to the pursuit of power. Unlike the early Chinese political treatises, the *Arthasastra* also dealt in considerable detail with problems of everyday state administration.

The Middle East also made its contribution, although at a later epoch, to the Mirror of Kings literature. Here, too, the wisdom books or aphorisms and counsels of Sa'di and of Nushirwan the Just gave place to more systematic manuals of political and personal conduct for the prince. Unlike the Chinese and Indian treatises, the *Mirror of Princes* of Ibn Iskandar also gave attention to questions of etiquette, recreation, love, the rearing of children, and the purchasing of slaves. The relations of minister (vizier) to the king and the art of selecting counselors are treated as part of the overall wisdom required for rule.

The Uses of History

The manuals of statecraft, important and numerous as they became, never supplanted a rival source of political guidance, also embodied in books, namely, historical writings. These two types of books were not viewed as competitors. On the contrary, the writers of manuals generally recommended historical reading to the prince as an important form of political education. Machiavelli, James VI, and Louis XIV all urged the prince and his counselors to be, in the words of King James, "well versed in authenticke histories, and

[43]Crump, 1970, p. 4.

in the Chronicles of all nations."[44] This recommendation was not confined to the manuals of statecraft. Rulers, statesmen, and most historians have shown substantial agreement on the political relevance of historical knowledge, and this is almost as true in modern times as in the past when fewer sources of advice and guidance were available.

The importance of history has seemed so self-evident to those who have insisted on its value for the ruler or his counselors that justification for this emphasis is often neglected. Nonetheless, a variety of uses of historical knowledge emerge from the frequent references to its importance. First of all, history is seen as providing an extension in time and space of the ruler's or counselor's own experience, and since experience is a major source of political wisdom, this extension of experience is of the first importance. Botero's statement brings out as well the convenience and pleasure of experiencing through history many instructive events without personal danger and expense. "Experience is of two kinds, being acquired either directly on one's own account, or indirectly through other people. The first kind is of necessity restricted both in time and space, for one man cannot be in many places nor have experience of many things. . . . The second kind is of two sorts, for a man may learn from the living or from the dead. Lessons learnt from the living may not extend far in time, but they embrace many places. . . . But a far greater field of study is provided by the writings of those who are already dead, for they cover the entire history of the world, in all its parts. History is the most pleasing theatre imaginable; for there a man learns for himself at the expense of others, there he can see shipwrecks without fear, war without danger, the customs and institutions of many nations without expense. There he descries the origins, means and ends and the causes of the growth and downfall of empires. . . ."[45] Commynes' statement is less systematic but perhaps more persuasive. "One of the surest ways of making a man wise [is] by reading ancient history and learning how to conduct and undertake one's affairs safely and wisely by the history and examples of our predecessors. For our life is so brief that it is not possible to have very many kinds of

[44]James VI, *Basilicon Doron*, vol. 1, p. 149.

[45]Botero, pp. 36–37.

experiences. In addition to this, as our lives are shorter than the lives of man used to be and our bodies are not so strong, so we are weaker in faith and loyalty towards one another. . . . [We] are more often than not surrounded by men who have an eye for nothing except to please their masters and to praise them for all their acts whether good or bad. . . . But wise princes and those who have read widely are never deceived by them nor are their councillors so foolhardy as to attempt to make them swallow lies."[46]

History provides insight and sensitivity that aid in the interpretation of current events and guide responses to them. A knowledge of history instills a form of wisdom. "My debt to history," wrote President Truman, "is one which cannot be calculated. . . . Reading history, to me, was far more than a romantic adventure. It was solid instruction and wise teaching. . . ."[47] Truman's lengthy statement on history in his *Memoirs* spells out very fully the value he derived from historical reading. Still, it is not easy for those convinced of the contribution that a knowledge of history has made to their political careers to give persuasive proof or to demonstrate its mode of operation. The process by which the mind reaches a decision on important affairs is often not known either to the decision maker himself or to observers of him, except where the decision-making process has been reduced to specific rules from which little or no deviation is permitted. Nonetheless the information, decision models, and values provided by historical understanding are hardly likely, in the eyes of statesmen who have such knowledge, to seem without pronounced consequences for their own behavior. Occasionally political figures have referred to

---

[46]Commynes, pp. 137–138. Historical knowledge is not only seen as extending personal experience, but personal experience, in its turn, is believed to deepen historical understanding. Polybius contended that it was hardly possible to write military history without military experience. Gibbon makes the same point concerning his military experience: "The captain of the Hampshire Grenadiers . . . had not been useless to the historian of the Roman Empire." Polybius also makes the point that in questioning witnesses of an event, the man without experience simply does not know how to put the right questions (Polybius, vol. 2, p. 116, and vol. 1, p. viii). Some modern historians, Meinecke, for example, and Marxists, have emphasized the contribution made to the historian by participation, even if only emotional, in political struggles.

[47]Truman, vol. 1, p. 119. Truman's rejection of history as a "romantic adventure" coincides with a similar rejection by Machiavelli and contrasts with John F. Kennedy's "romantic sense of history" (Schlesinger, 1965, p. 78).

parallels between a past situation and one that they face, and have stated or implied that this awareness became the source of a political idea or a decision. When Colonel House speculated on the possibility of forcing the antagonists in World War I to accept United States mediation by threatening that the United States would join the war against that side which was unwilling to lay down its arms, it was from "a striking historical parallel which came to him from his historical reading."[48] John Adams, in September 1776, at a time of considerable military difficulty, drew lessons from Polybius concerning the handling of troops and felt that "perhaps there is not in all Antiquity, if there is in universal History, an Example more apposite to our Situation than that of Thebes. . . ."[49]

Aristotle believed that the narration in popular assemblies of past events enables the listeners to make better plans for the future.[50] To Polybius historical knowledge was indispensable for supplying the precedents necessary for acquiring allies and ensuring their cooperation.[51] It was from history that Machiavelli derived one of his principal theorems, namely, that mercenary armies are dangerous and a republic more readily survives when defended by its own citizens.[52]

Perhaps the most frequent claim on behalf of historical knowledge as applied to politics is its ability to facilitate the prediction of events or trends. "It is by applying analogies to our own circumstances," wrote Polybius, "that we get the means and basis for calculating the future. . . ."[53] "If your plans fail," warned Motse, "learn the future from the past. . . ."[54] The "past resembles the future more than one drop of water another," wrote Ibn Khaldun.[55] "History repeats itself and men remain the same," Machiavelli wrote to his friend Guicciardini.[56] To write history as an aid to

---

[48]In 1813 Austria offered to mediate between Napoleon and the allied governments, intimating that if this offer were rejected by Napoleon, she would join his enemies. Seymour, vol. 2, p. 85, n. 1.

[49]John Adams, vol. 3, p. 439.

[50]Aristotle, *Rhetoric*, bk. III, 1417^{b}.

[51]Polybius, vol. 1, p. 192.

[52]Machiavelli, *The Prince*, p. 46.

[53]Polybius, vol. 2, p. 102.

[54]Hughes, p. 58.

[55]Ibn Khaldun, *The Muqaddimah*, vol. 1, p. 17.

[56]Machiavelli, "Choix de lettres," in *Le Prince*, p. 241.

understanding the future, says Thucydides, was his goal: "If it be judged useful by those inquirers who desire an exact knowledge of the past, as an aid to the interpretation of the future, which in the course of human things must resemble if it does not reflect it, I shall be content."[57]

Perhaps the boldest and most self-confident claim to infer future events from history was made not by a statesman or historian but by Samuel Taylor Coleridge referring to his work as a political journalist:

> On every great occurrence I endeavoured to discover in past history the event that most nearly resembled it. I procured, wherever it was possible, the contemporary historians, memorialists, and pamphleteers. Then fairly subtracting the points of difference from those of likeness, as the balance favoured the former or the latter, I conjectured that the result would be the same or different. . . . Armed with the two-fold knowledge of history and the human mind, a man will scarcely err in his judgment concerning the sum total of any future national event, if he have been able to procure the original documents of the past, together with authentic accounts of the present, and if he have a philosophic tact for what is truly important in facts. . . .[58]

The claims of poets ought not to be lightly treated. In his work on political prophecies, the historian H.A.L. Fisher pays a tribute to Coleridge's friend Wordsworth: "For the higher gifts of divination which depend upon an insight into the fundamental moral forces and aspects of the world, Wordsworth was superior to either Pitt or Napoleon."[59]

Botero, to emphasize the value of history, pointed out that even military skills, normally the product of long experience, can be acquired by the study of history.[60]

John Adams felt that his interventions on military matters required no apology since "I had read as much on the military Art and much more of the History of War than any American Officer of that Army, General Lee excepted."[61]

---

[57]Thucydides, p. xvii.

[58]Coleridge, *Biographia Literaria*, p. 115. Coleridge refers here to articles he wrote for *The Morning Post* and *The Courier*. Coleridge was also the author of *The Statesman's Manual; or, the Bible the Best Guide to Political Skill and Foresight* (1816).

[59]Fisher, pp. 3–30.

[60]Botero, p. 37.

[61]John Adams, vol. 3, p. 446

President Truman stressed that a main motive for reading a book, and more especially an historical book, is to get a better insight into people. Whether in fact he derived his ability in this respect from history is not subject to demonstration, but Secretary of State Acheson has affirmed "by understanding what men had done in the past he was able with a sometimes terrifying reality to anticipate what a man would do in the present. He had an almost unbelievable ability to judge character."[62] At the very least, a knowledge of history may spare one from being unduly surprised by events. President Truman expressed this in the aphorism: "The only thing new in the world is the history you don't know."[63]

The praise of history as a source of counsel has not been unanimous. Part of this reserve has been due not so much to a depreciation of historical writings as of some classes of scholars who made use of them. Rulers and their counselors emphasized the importance of experience and were critical of persons who discussed political affairs largely on the basis of book knowledge. Such persons were especially viewed as pedants if they were addicted to an uncritical adulation of the past. The Chinese realist writers like Lord Shang and Han Fei Tzu were particularly critical of Confucian preoccupation with the great emperors of ancient times as guides to present policy. Similar arguments were made by Richelieu who criticized those who think that they can run a kingdom by maxims derived from their books. "The past," wrote Richelieu, "is not the same as the present, and the character of times, of places, and of persons is different."[64] Richelieu's comparison of past and present was, no doubt, sincerely meant, but it seems clear that his point was largely made to strengthen his criticism of scholars without practical experience. Elsewhere he recommended the study of history as important for the ruler.

Bacon had similar reservations concerning the study of the past, but he was critical not so much of scholars and pedants in general as of lawyers and jurists who carried over into politics their addiction to the study of precedents and who sought in past authorities support for present policies. But this did not mean, any

---

[62]Miller, pp. 24 and 378–379.

[63]Ibid., p. 70.

[64]Richelieu, *Testament Politique*, p. 289.

more than for Richelieu, that history could be disregarded as a source of counsel and political education. Bacon was learned in history, continually drew on his historical knowledge, and was himself an historian, author of a life of Henry VII.

History was also viewed as having limited value to guide political decisions by those who emphasized the role of fortune, that is, of chance and the unpredictable. But the importance attributed to chance was itself largely justified through the study of history and the frequent decisive interventions of the unforeseeable there recorded.

Depreciation of the role of historical knowledge in political guidance stemmed, too, from a desire to strike out into new paths and to avoid reciting over and over again the famous examples drawn from historians. The historians themselves developed reservations concerning their role. Jacques Cujas, one of the great jurists and scholars of the sixteenth century, marked a departure toward a new professionalism in his conviction that it was his task to teach history and not to draw from it lessons for either the present or the future.[65] Erasmus was certainly not disposed to eliminate history from the reading of the prince but he preferred works of a high ethical content such as the Bible, Aristotle, Plato, Cicero, and Plutarch. As much as he admired the classics, he did not think that even they should be followed slavishly: "But indeed since the whole scene of human affairs has been overturned, who today can talk sensibly unless he uses language very different from that of Cicero? Wherever I turn my eyes, I see all things changed, I stand before another stage and I behold a different play, nay, even a different world."[66] This moderated his enthusiasm for history as a source of political guidance, but there was an additional reason for his reservations. History portrays both evil and good men and the prince runs the danger of succumbing to the evil models. "Herodotus and Xenophon were both pagans and often set forth the worst types of prince. . . . Sallust and Livy . . . approve some things which are by no means to be approved for a Christian prince. When you hear about Achilles, Xerxes, Cyrus, Darius, and Julius Caesar . . . you are hearing about great raging robbers. . . ."[67]

[65]Gilmore, p. 37.
[66]Cited by Gilmore, pp. 103–104.
[67]Erasmus, *Education of a Christian Prince*, p. 201.

The reservations expressed on the political utility of historical knowledge did not go unchallenged. Machiavelli sought in his *Prince* and especially in *The Discourses* to preserve history from misuses which could bring it into disrepute. His statement that it is easy, by diligent study of the past, to foresee what is likely to happen in the future in any republic was a commonplace in the early sixteenth century.[68] But Machiavelli did not concede that in employing history for this purpose he was following a well-worn path: "I have decided," he wrote in *The Discourses,* "to enter on a path which up to now has been trodden by no one. . . ." This claim is based on his conviction that the majority of those who read history do so to derive pleasure from the narrative and are not seriously engaged in extracting the sense of it and savoring the knowledge it contains.[69] The benefit of history cannot be derived from a passive scholarship but only by intensive analysis of carefully chosen cases. In brief, it was by transforming history into comparative history, or perhaps in contemporary terms, into political sociology or political science, that Machiavelli sought to extract its hidden lessons.[70]

Similarly Machiavelli's contemporary, Guicciardini, a highly experienced statesman and one of the great historians of his age, noted in his *Ricordi* that "Past events throw light on future events, because the world has always been the same as it now is, and all it is now, or shall be hereafter, has been in time past. Things accordingly repeat themselves, but . . . it is not everyone who can recognize them but only he who is discerning and who notes and considers them diligently."[71] But Guicciardini also wrote, perhaps alluding to Machiavelli's use of Roman history, "To judge by example is very misleading. Unless they are similar in every respect, examples are useless, since every tiny difference in the case may be a cause of great variations in the effects. And to discern these

---

[68]Hale, p. xxiv.

[69]Machiavelli, *The Discourses*, pp. 103–105.

[70]Machiavelli's "political sociology" or "political science" would, of course, have been based on a close study of far-ranging historical materials and not on the cursory knowledge of history that often does duty in contemporary social sciences dominated by the immediate national scene and by the laudable ambition to provide quantitative demonstrations.

[71]Hale, p. xxiv.

tiny differences takes a good and perspicacious eye."[72] Since no two historical situations will fail to diverge in one particular or another, Guicciardini's statement, if taken literally, would contradict his earlier statement and destroy all possibility of using history to arrive at anticipations of the future.

The use of history to guide political action is still debated today. Ernest R. May has argued that misleading ideas about the "lessons" of modern history influenced United States policy in the Cold War, Korea, and Vietnam. Nonetheless he believes that a more judicious use of history and historians by government officials would benefit government.[73] Henry Kissinger has defended the relevance of history against the charge that the uniqueness of historical events precludes arriving at general conclusions: "Whatever relationship exists depends, not on a precise correspondence, but on a similarity of the problems confronted. And the conclusions will reflect—just as with any other generalization—the ability to abstract some of the uniqueness of individual experience."[74] This defense of history as a source of political inspiration is not surprising in a political adviser and statesman who has said, "I think of myself as a historian more than as a statesman."[75] Konrad Adenauer reproached a modern historian who, in the spirit of Jacques Cujas, affirmed to Adenauer that it was not the business of the historian to foresee events. "I do not demand prophecy of a historian, but I think that his work—especially if he is a modern historian—is not complete until he has tried to predict future developments from present events. . . ."[76]

The Adviser as Educator

It is evident that practically all of the advisory literature available to rulers—proverbs, maxims, fables, wisdom books, Mirrors of Kings, manuals of statecraft, and historical works—were intended to educate the ruler in the general principles of his craft and not

---

[72]Guicciardini, *Maxims*, p. 71.
[73]Ernest R. May. See also M. I. Finley.
[74]Henry Kissinger, 1957, p. 331.
[75]Kissinger, 1974, p. 629.
[76]Adenauer, p. 15.

to advise him on specific problems of foreign and domestic policy faced by his state or principality. To be sure, Charles V, in the communications he prepared for his son, dealt, along with more general matters, with specific questions of Spanish foreign policy; and Richelieu, in his political testament addressed to Louis XIII, discussed French policy towards Spain. But these, on the whole, are exceptional excursions into the realm of immediate problems.

The process of educating the prince and molding his character could hardly be left to the printed page alone, especially in the younger years of the prince. Where hereditary rule existed, the 'choice' of a good ruler was reduced to the possibility of perfecting him and this in its turn often rested on the choice of his tutor, which was therefore viewed as a matter of the first importance. "A King without training," wrote the anonymous author of a fourteenth century Mirror of Kings, "is like a fool with a sword in his hand. . . ."[77] Already in the ninth century, Hincmar of Rheims had prepared for Louis the Bald not only his *Instruction of a New King in the Correct Administration of a Kingdom* but also his *The Establishment of Suitable Tutors and Advisors for the Royal Sons of Louis the Bald*.[78]

The role of the political adviser as an educator is reflected in very literal fashion in the frequency with which political advisers were also tutors to princes. In feudal China the class of men called *ju*, of which Confucius was a notable member, were tutors to the princes and lordlings of the feudal states; their role as political advisers was an outgrowth of these tutorial relations. Shang Yang, architect of the foreign and domestic policies of Ch'in, and of its conquest and unification of the Warring States, got his start as tutor to the young princes of Wei. Similarly, in India, the Brahman, Kautilya, as mentioned earlier, started out as the mentor and then became chief minister to Chandragupta, founder of the Maurya dynasty (321 B.C.). In Greece, Aristotle, tutor to Alexander for four years, continued his influence through his nephew Callisthenes, placed in the service of Alexander when the latter departed on his Indian expedition. In Rome, Seneca was tutor to the 12-year-old boy who was to become the Emperor Nero. After Nero's accession,

---

[77]Born, 1928a, p. 494.

[78]Born, 1965, p. 106. See also p. 12, p. 31 and pp. 141–144 for Erasmus' views concerning the importance, selection, and character of the royal tutor.

Seneca became his unofficial first minister and together with his military friend Burrus procured for Rome five of its most distinguished years of imperial rule. Cornelius Fronto, teacher of the young Marcus Aurelius, continued his influence over his student well into the latter's mature years. The eleventh-century scholar Gerbert had the good fortune to be the teacher of not one but two future crowned heads: Otto III, emperor of Germany, and Robert Capet, King of France. Gerbert ascended in power together with his two charges and became Pope Sylvester II. Botero, Hobbes, and Don Juan Manuel all served as tutors to princes and continued the relation at court in later years.

Few princes were fortunate enough to have the first minister of their country as a tutor during their childhood. Louis XIV, however, during the years of his minority received instruction from Cardinal Mazarin whom Richelieu had selected to succeed him. When Louis was fourteen or fifteen, Mazarin spent a period almost every day discussing with the young boy the current problems of state. He reviewed the dispatches of the day and urged Louis to read the necessary documents and to formulate his own ideas in writing. Mazarin had Louis attend those meetings of the council of state at which relatively simple problems were to be discussed. How well Mazarin's system of instruction succeeded is reflected by Louis' practice, passed on to his own son, of "reasoning alone and by myself" on state problems to discover whether his first thoughts "were the same as those reached by able and experienced men." In the last year of Mazarin's life, the Venetian ambassador informed his government that Mazarin's sessions with the young Louis sometimes lasted hours on end so that "one cannot doubt that, if he does not fall under the influence of another minister, he will become a very great prince." Mazarin apparently had confidence in the training he had provided for he recommended to Louis that he act as his own first minister.[79]

Many kings who could not boast of having had, while princes, such great minds as Aristotle, Seneca, or Erasmus as their tutors, were able to indulge their vanity, curiosity, or genuine devotion to high intellectual accomplishments by attaching to their persons and courts, sometimes almost as prisoners, the leading intellectuals

---

[79]For this account of the relations between Mazarin and Louis, see Wolf, pp. 60–77.

of their age. Voltaire at the court of Frederick the Great, Descartes at that of Queen Christina, and Diderot at the court of Catherine the Great are familiar examples.

The adviser to the ruler is often caught up in problems of domestic and foreign policy and may have little time or inclination to devote himself to the ruler's political education. Nonetheless, he will have an interest in trying to provide him with more than advice on specific issues since it will facilitate his own task if the ruler understands the principles that lie behind his recommendations on individual matters. To this extent he will be like Patronio, counselor to Count Lucanor, who whenever he is asked for advice on a specific matter, counters with a story that can be translated into a general rule of action and thereby serve on future occasions as well. Thus, Patronio not only advises, he educates.

Where we have, as in the case of Joinville's chronicle of Louis IX's crusade, a reasonably detailed account of the behavior of an actual adviser, one notes how, in the manner of Patronio, Joinville seems to intersperse general principles of political wisdom with his advice on specific decisions. When the Abbot of Cluny presented King Louis with two expensive palfreys prior to engaging him in a business discussion, Joinville used the occasion to instruct King Louis on an important point: "When the abbot had departed, I came to the king, and said: 'I should like to ask, if it so pleases you, whether you have given ear to the Abbot of Cluny with the more favour because of those two palfreys that he gave you yesterday?' The king thought a long time, and then said: 'Truly, yes. 'Sire,' I continued, 'do you know why I have asked you this question?' 'Why?' said he. 'Because, sire,' I replied, 'I advise and counsel that, when you return to France, you forbid all your sworn councillors to accept aught from those who have matters to bring before you.'"[80]

Emphasis on the political education of the prince was intended to make him capable of accurate and independent judgment. The adviser's interest in pursuing a consistent policy required a principal who was neither scatterbrained nor uninterested. Commynes remarked with some emotion: "Believe me, God did not establish the office of King or of any other prince to be exercised by igno-

[80]Joinville, pp. 300–301.

ramuses or by those who glory in saying, 'I'm not a clerk, I leave my council to take care of such matters, I trust them,' and then, without more ado, go off to have a good time. . . . I think God cannot send a greater plague on a country than an unintelligent prince."[81] For Bacon, too, the fact that the king was responsible to no one meant not only that he must be aided by wise counselors but must be wise himself. The notion that the leader need not be as capable or instructed as those who serve him and that the art of government, for the leader, reduces to the science of personnel selection seems, then, to be a relatively modern view. I do not know what the true history of this notion is, but the first clear expression of it that I have found is in Vauvenargues (1745): "In high places it is, perhaps, more useful to know and to be willing to make use of well-trained people than to be one oneself."[82]

The distinction between the adviser who educates and the adviser who confines advice to particular solutions for immediate issues is still relevant in modern times but decreasingly so. Cánovas del Castillo, statesman of the Spanish Restoration of 1874, did not forget his early background as a provincial schoolmaster and did not content himself with advising Alfonso XII on specific political and constitutional issues. The young king was made to read Walter Bagehot and such other treatises as Cánovas deemed would properly instruct him in his role as monarch.[83] In our own day we find Walter W. Heller, former chairman of the president's Council of Economic Advisers, emphasizing that in economic affairs advice on specific questions of economic policy does not suffice. "Experience of recent years has demonstrated that education . . . of the President . . . is an inescapable part of an economic adviser's function. The explanatory and analytical models of the economist must be implanted—at least intuitively—. . . if economic advice is to be accepted and translated into action."[84] Under the heading, "The Education of Gerald Ford," *Time* magazine reported that a newly appointed consultant to President Ford was "styling" the president's education through a series of seven or eight dinners annually

[81]Commynes, p. 138.
[82]Vauvenargues, p. 128.
[83]Carr, pp. 348–349.
[84]Heller, p. 31.

to each of which a few prominent intellectuals are invited, thus enabling the president "to reflect on the broader historical and philosophical contexts of his decisions."[85]

Nonetheless, it is a major restriction today on the role of advisers that they only infrequently exercise broadly educational functions and must, on the whole, confine themselves to advice on a succession of specific issues. Partly, of course, the contrast in this respect between the early and later history of the adviser and his principal is due to the difference between, on the one hand, a prince who had to be trained and educated for his position and, on the other hand, a politician or high administrator who is presumed to have reached his post by virtue of already having the requisite capabilities and therefore to require assistance largely with respect to technical matters that are the province of highly specialized experts. But there is another reason why today the adviser often has little opportunity to function as an educator: this is his reduced level of access to his principal. Naturally, an adviser who sees his principal only intermittently or provides his advice in a brief position paper must generally confine himself to giving advice on specific problems or on matters of his particular expertise. In previous ages, the adviser was much more likely to have continuous access and fewer persons to compete with. He could, therefore, more readily combine advice on specific issues with broader educational efforts.

Councils

The image of the political adviser is that of an individual, but from ancient times until today advisory functions have been performed not only by individuals but by groups—councils, cabinets, assemblies, parties, committees, commissions, boards, institutes, and 'think tanks,' among others.

The council was often a rival center of power rather than a source of counsel for the ruler. Early kingship was generally a form of shared rather than absolute power. The Spartan kings, essentially military and religious leaders, had no real control over the Spartan councils. In France, in the early Middle Ages, the king governed

[85] *Time*, December 23, 1974, p. 10.

with a council whose membership he could not entirely control and without whose approval his acts lost their legal force. By the fifteenth century, however, the king's council tended to divide into specialized sections. Only those counselors chosen by the king played an important role, and the Great Council was transformed into a small council attached to his person. Thus, the council was changed from a center of power to the king's personal advisory instrument. This, of course, did not prevent the small council from acquiring considerable power if a king, like Francis I, was willing to let it rule in his place.[86]

Similarly, in England, both feudal principles and early Germanic traditions combined to limit the king's power by that of the great men of the realm. In the twelfth and early thirteenth centuries, the magna curia regis was more often engaged in debating matters of war, peace, and taxation than in acting as a trial court.[87] But increasingly advice for the king came from counselors he selected to attend him, and the magna curia became primarily a court. It was, perhaps, the forerunner of Parliament which even in the sixteenth and early seventeenth centuries was still largely thought of as a court rather than as a legislative or advisory body. The struggle of Parliament in the early seventeenth century to assert itself was in part an attack on the king's right to have personal advisers who did not possess the confidence of Parliament.[88]

A council whose sole function is to advise the sovereign is not, as Hobbes pointed out, "a Public Person," since its advice is addressed to the sovereign alone. But it inevitably acquires some administrative functions since "in a Monarchy, they represent the Monarch, in delivering his Commands to the Publique Ministers."[89]

'Council' suggests a formally constituted body but initially the king's council was often simply those who were with him on a particular occasion or who at a particular time accompanied him on his travels through the kingdom. Joinville's famous description of Louis IX seated under a tree at Vincennes reflects this infor-

---

[86]Bontems, p. 62.

[87]Turner, pp. 167–168.

[88]Gooch, pp. 65–68.

[89]Hobbes, p. 129. This is parallel to the administrative or executive functions and missions of the president's personal White House advisers noted above, pp. 17–18.

mality.[90] The composition of the king's council was fluid and it was only in the course of time that it was transformed into a body with a recognized membership and a recognized head, as in Richelieu's time in France. But this more stable council still owed its existence to the king's pleasure and was attached to his person. When the council was composed, as under Louis XIV, of ministers responsible for particular departments of the king's government, it took on the character of a cabinet with heavy administrative as well as advisory functions. In Britain, meetings of the cabinet were presided over by the king until the accession of the Hanoverian George I ended the practice simply because his knowledge of English was inadequate.[91]

The council of war is one of the most frequent forms in which the council appears in historical narrative, and this signifies that the risks of life and death, of personal and collective honor could not generally be taken without consultation with those whose lives and honor were at stake. When Jason assembled his Argonauts in council, he said, "Sharing the danger as we do, we share the right of speech. . . ."[92] The gravity of the issues often meant that a common deliberation and agreement were involved and not simply expressions of advice to the leader. But the extent to which the elements of assent and advice were mixed was determined in part by the political habitudes of the society at large and by the authority of the military leader of the moment. When Xenophon's council of war rejected their leader's proposal to prepare, on the last stages of their homeward journey, for an overland march rather than a sea crossing, Xenophon refrained from putting the matter to a vote, hoping to enforce his preference by other means.[93] But when Xerxes held a council of war to decide whether to attack the Greeks, his response to advice in the negative clearly showed that the council of war was simply intended to confirm his own decision.[94] Prior to the battle of Agincourt the French king assembled his council

---

[90]Joinville, pp. 149–150.

[91]The king's place at the cabinet meeting was taken by the senior minister, but the term 'prime minister' did not come into general use until the nineteenth century and even today is not established in British law. Nicolson, p. 111.

[92]*The Voyage of Argo*, p. 114.

[93]Xenophon, *Anabasis*, pp. 318–320.

[94]Herodotus, pp. 394–395.

"to the number of five and thirty, [and] asked their advice what was to be done. . . . At length thirty of them agreed that the Englishmen should not depart unfought withal, and five were of a contrary opinion, but the greater number ruled the matter. . . ."[95] On the other hand, when the council of war called by Louis IX strongly advised abandoning the crusade and returning to France, Louis followed the opinion of a small minority and especially the judgment of his young counselor Joinville.[96]

The councils of democratic or republican polities were generally political assemblies and centers of power rather than simply advisory instruments. But republican institutions often concealed the concentration of power in the hands of a few individuals so that republican councils frequently were reduced to advisory bodies rather than being deliberating assemblies sharing the power to make decisions. Often, too, the multiplication of councils, as in Florence, by fragmenting their power reduced it. Special problems often led to the formation of an ad hoc council, in Florence called the *pratica*, whose functions were purely advisory. These councils sometimes had functions similar to those of presidential or royal commissions in contemporary Anglo-Saxon practice.

In the modern world the proliferation of specialized knowledge and techniques increased enormously the role of advisory services in the polity. Political assemblies themselves, such as the House of Commons and Congress, long ago developed a committee system to permit specialization in the consideration of legislative problems. In England, early manifestations of a permanent committee system had already appeared in the sixteenth-century House of Commons.[97]

In the contemporary world, it is not in political assemblies but in other institutions that the vast proliferation and specialization of technical advisory services most strikingly manifests itself. In 1972, Congress, alarmed at the growth of advisory committees attached to the Executive branch, passed the Federal Committees Act (PL92–463, 1972). This Act required all such committees to report on their activities, and in 1973 the Committee on Government

---

[95]Holinshed, p. 552a.
[96]Joinville, pp. 240–243.
[97]Bradshaw and Pring, p. 208.

Operations of the Senate issued *Federal Advisory Committees* in four volumes and 5,703 pages. In the mid-sixties, the president's eyes and ears abroad, his representatives and advisers, that is his ambassadors,[98] were sending 400,000 words per day by telegraph and, of course, a far vaster flow of information by non-telegraphic means.[99]

Presidents frequently call on ad hoc commissions, committees, and 'task forces' to provide advice on special problems.[100] Prior to his inauguration John F. Kennedy had twenty-nine 'task forces' working for him on foreign and domestic problems.[101]

When issues requiring advice are highly technical and the problems are of great import, it is natural for advisers to the ruler to require advisers for themselves; thus, the advisory system becomes a pyramid. President Truman found that the National Security Council which he had organized was becoming too large and cumbersome because *his* advisers were bringing *their* advisers to the meetings.[102] Increasingly, the pyramid of advisory services rests on a foundation of corporate enterprises specializing in the provision of research, analysis, and recommendations on policy issues—nonprofit organizations such as the Rand Corporation and the Brookings Institution, together with similar enterprises organized for profit. Many of these work or initially worked in specialized areas such as defense, but others, more especially the commercial management consultant enterprises, serve a wide range of commercial, industrial, and governmental interests. Management consultant firms in the United States numbered 400 in 1940 and 3,000 in 1970. More than one-third of the receipts of Booz, Allen, and Hamilton, probably the third largest management consultant

---

[98]That the ambassador is a personal representative of the president is sometimes forgotten. When Franklin D. Roosevelt wanted to refer in a speech to Joseph P. Kennedy as "my ambassador" he was advised by his speechwriter to change it to "our ambassador" but refused to do so on the defensible ground that United States ambassadors were indeed *his* ambassadors. Sherwood, p. 191. This also provides some justification for Roosevelt's instruction to an ambassador to communicate directly with him and not through the State Department. Bailey, p. 10.

[99]Bailey, p. 65.

[100]An excellent summary of these advisory services, together with a bibliography, can be found in Cronin and Greenberg.

[101]Schlesinger, 1965, pp. 155–160.

[102]Truman, vol. 2, p. 59.

firm in the United States, came in 1972 from federal, state, and local governments.[103] Management consultant firms then employed about fifty to sixty thousand persons, presumably inclusive of nonprofessional personnel. Adding those in policy-oriented research in nonprofit institutes, in universities, in government agencies, and private industry, it is apparent that policy-oriented analysts or advisers constitute in the United States a very sizable group. It is not surprising, then, that this has led to the growth of special educational institutes, departments, or schools, for the training of policy analysts. The existence of these schools at a graduate level, together with the development of specialized associations and journals for policy analysts, testifies to the rapid professionalization of the advisory services provided to government and private enterprise.

The provision of advice by committee, the tendency for decision making to become a group effort, has consequences of capital importance for the decision-making process. Some of these were already noted by the Greeks whose experience with political assemblies alerted them to problems of collective decision making. The use of councils, except those of the most severely limited size, as a forum for discussion and deliberation rather than as a means for soliciting individual expressions of opinion, was viewed with alarm as a perversion of the decision-making process by Guicciardini and particularly by Hobbes. In our own day, Dean Acheson and Henry Kissinger have equally expressed some antipathy for and concern over the contemporary organization of political advice. We shall return to these criticisms in a later context. Here we have wanted only to draw attention to the council, the committee, and other advisory groups, as one among many forms in which advisory functions have been performed.

---

[103]Stanford Research Institute, formerly a nonprofit corporation, and Planning Research Corporation are the two largest firms in the field. Henry Allen, "Consultants Have All the Answers," *Los Angeles Times*, September 2, 1973.

3

Selection

Seleucus I, king of Syria, used to say that if people knew what a job it was just to read and write so many letters, they wouldn't even bother to pick up a crown that had been thrown away.[1] This formulation of the burdens of kingship underlines one of the prime requirements for those who would serve the king—literacy. It was, of course, not simply correspondence, but also various forms of administrative, fiscal, judicial, and other record keeping that opened to those who were literate and numerate pathways to the court and to power.

Churchmen, Lawyers, and Doctors

In the early Middle Ages, literacy meant above all the clergy or clerical class, the principal members of European Christian society—with the exception of the poets—who had a substantial degree

[1]Plutarch, *Moralia*, vol. X, p. 113.

of literacy. From Constantinople to Ireland churchmen became the counselors and administrative aides of kings and princes. An account of a ninth-century meeting of the eastern emperor's council shows almost all the spokesmen to be ecclesiastics.[2] Even in the more recently and thinly Christianized regions, such as the British Isles, churchmen were the principal advisers of the Saxon kings and formed their secretariats.

It was not only a utilitarian, scribal skill that gave to churchmen their powerful role in political life. Some churchmen were members of influential families. Second, the religious sentiments of many kings in the early Middle Ages—it was not at all unknown for rulers to abandon their thrones in order to end their days as monks—favored an important role for churchmen as royal advisers. The churchman as confessor and spiritual director was readily transformed into a political adviser, a transformation made all the easier in a period when the Church was an important political force. Third, churchmen were proficient in nonecclesiastical fields such as civil law and provided professional skills that only later became available from other professional groups. Even after the Norman conquest in 1066, lawyers were virtually nonexistent in England. Fourth, the situation of other groups that were actual or potential rivals for the positions held by churchmen favored the success of the latter. This is particularly clear in the case of the barons who had the strongest claims to counsel the king and to stand at his right hand.[3] The barons, apart from their ignorance of letters, were preoccupied with their castles and lands and their own retainers and could not attend the king with the regularity or continuity of churchmen and clerks who were freer to reside at the court and to follow the king in his movements about his realm.

Alfred, King of Wessex, met this difficulty by having his older and experienced thegns who were his advisers serve him one month in three thus giving them time to oversee their estates.[4] In time of war, the nobles asserted a greater leadership, although churchmen

---

[2]Runciman, p. 67.

[3]Among the Franks, to be sure, the leading men were often officials and advisers as well as warriors—Mayor of the Palace, the Marshal, the Counts of the Palace, the Treasurer, but the Secretary was "almost always a Gaul, since an educated Frank was very exceptional." Norman, p. 22.

[4]Ibid., p. 72.

were not excluded from councils of war, nor, in some cases, from acting as warrior-priests as did Archbishop Turpin in the *Song of Roland*. The Synod of Westminster of 1175 ruled that the clergy should not bear arms but chroniclers continued to be scandalized for many years by fighting clerics.[5] The statesmen who stood at the side of their kings were, then, in many instances churchmen like Barbarossa's chancellor Reginald von Dassel, Archbishop of Cologne, or Lanfranc who accompanied William the Conqueror to England and became Archbishop of Canterbury. In the Norwegian *King's Mirror* we read: "Whenever kings meet, there the best men are always assembled; for the kings bring their chief men with them to such conferences: archbishops, bishops, earls, landedmen, and hirdmen or knights."[6] It is evident that rank is implied by this ordering in which churchmen come first. Botero, writing four hundred years later, still attaches great importance, in the work of government, to constant consultation with prelates.[7] It is useful to recall that when, in 1529, Sir Thomas More reluctantly succeeded Cardinal Wolsey as Lord Chancellor of England, he was the *first* layman to hold that high office; and that in France under Louis XIII, during the early years of Louis XIV, and during the reign of Louis XV, three cardinals, Richelieu, Mazarin, and Fleury were the first ministers of the realm.

Although the Church was generally pleased to have churchmen in positions of great secular power, it was less pleased at the ease with which those in holy and minor orders used their near monopoly of literacy to desert religious duties and posts and to attach themselves to the courts of the powerful. The Council of Paris of 829 noted, "An unhappy custom has arisen . . . that many subject to ecclesiastical rule . . . make their way wherever their desire persuadeth them. They are received not only by bishops and abbots, but by counts and nobles. It is entreated, and the imperial power appealed to, that no layman shall receive a clerk of this kind." And again, the civil powers are asked "that monks, priests and clerks be discouraged from coming about the palace."[8] More than five

---

[5]Ibid., p. 134

[6]*The King's Mirror*, p. 178.

[7]Botero, p. x.

[8]Cited in Waddell, p. 277.

hundred years later William Langland could still complain in the Prologue to his *Piers the Ploughman* that "Bishops and novices, Doctors of Divinity and other great divines—. . . I saw them all living in London, even in Lent. Some took posts at Court counting the king's money, or in the Courts of Exchequer and Chancery. . . ."

The churchman at the right hand of the king was not unique to Christendom although his extraordinary temporal power was hardly reproduced elsewhere. In India, the king's chaplain and other Brahman advisers were mentors in temporal as well as spiritual matters. In ancient China no similar ecclesiastical class existed but just as the clergy were often able in the West to displace the barons as the principal advisers and aids to the Christian kings, so too in feudal China the old nobility was displaced first by a class of retainers, men not of noble birth but possessed of some talents, and later by a class of specialists in government, men who were rhetoricians and "persuaders."[9]

In the latter half of the twelfth century, the growth in economic activity and the development of new legal institutions gave prominence to a rising class of jurists whose prestige began to rival that of the theologians and who were often able to displace churchmen as advisers and as administrators of the king's affairs. This displacement of churchmen by jurists was peculiar to Christendom, for in Islam and Israel law was scarcely distinguishable from theology and hardly a rival to it.[10] On the other hand, it appears that in Islam medically trained philosophers were highly respected at the courts of Moslem rulers.[11]

The role of the lawyer as a political adviser has grown enormously in the contemporary world, and nowhere so evidently as in the United States. Four of the eight secretaries of state in the Republican administrations from Theodore Roosevelt to Eisenhower were Wall Street lawyers: Elihu Root, Charles Evans Hughes, Henry Stimson, and John Foster Dulles. Democratic administrations have used lawyers equally freely both as official and unofficial advisers—Dean

---

[9]Crump, 1964, p. 4.

[10]Sarton, vol. II, pt.1, p. 318.

[11]Doctors have played a limited role in the political life of the West. The appointment of Dr. David Owen to the British Labour cabinet as foreign secretary in 1977 marks a recent exception to the general rule.

Acheson, Abe Fortas, James Rowe, Clark Clifford, Thomas Corcoran, George Ball, to name only a few.[12]

In societies governed by popular assemblies oratorical skill played an important role in providing access to high office and influence. The adviser required the ability not so much to move the mind of a single leader as the minds of an often disorderly assembly. Cleon, addressing his fellow Athenians, berated them for listening to speakers as if they were contestants or actors in a play. The assembly are "slaves to the pleasure of the ear, and more like the audience of a rhetorician than the council of a city."[13] Contemporary democracy places a similar premium on fluency and rhetorical ability, and this expresses itself in the importance of the press conference and the TV appearance as well as in the dependence many presidents have on their aides and advisers who serve as speech writers. Persons skilled in the craft of writing sometimes emerge, as did Robert E. Sherwood, in a position close to the president. The adviser often serves as a speech writer, as did Judge Rosenman for President Roosevelt and Theodore Sorensen for John F. Kennedy.

Youth and Age

When Gilgamesh, the young king of Uruk, "Uruk of the strong walls," in Mesopotamia, set out some four or more thousand years ago, together with his equally young friend and devoted companion Enkidu, to conquer the giant Humbaba in the great cedar forest he inhabited, the counselors of Uruk gathered in the marketplace to dissuade their young king from this foolhardy enterprise.[14] Gilgamesh scoffed at their advice and together with Enkidu set off for the cedar forest. Thus already in man's earliest literary record the counselors of the king emerge not only to play their traditional

[12]Joseph Kraft, pp. 150–151.

[13]Thucydides, p. 165

[14]The probable historical elements lying behind the epic are: the existence of Gilgamesh as king in Uruk; his reputation as a great builder of walls and temples; his need for the timber of the cedar forests of Amanus in north Syria or of Elam in southwest Persia; and the necessity to battle the strange tribes, and their gods, who possessed these forests. *The Epic of Gilgamesh*, pp. 30 and 54.

role as advisers, but also to establish for the first time an important theme that has persisted through four thousand years down to the present day: the conflict between the impetuousness and daring of a young ruler and the caution and hesitations of his older and more experienced advisers.

The persistence of this theme stems not only from the common disparagement of youth as lacking in experience and restraint, but from the aggravation of these deficiencies occasioned by a royal succession. The young ruler is a new ruler and he often replaces, as did Gilgamesh with Enkidu, his father's counselors with his young companions. This theme repeats itself in another early document, the biblical account of Rehoboam's dismissal of the advisers of his father, Solomon, and their replacement by men of his own age. "But he forsook the counsel of the old men, which they had given him, and consulted with the young men that were grown up with him."[15] This became the *locus classicus* for discussion of the problem.

It was not a mere knowledge of such ancient examples that kept this theme alive. Later writers who deal with the question are clearly impressed by contemporary experiences with the problem, as was the anonymous Norwegian author of *The King's Mirror* who traced political decline, after the death of a king, to "young counselors [who] come into the places of the old and wise advisers. . . ."[16] Commynes deplored, especially in connection with negotiation, the tendency of young princes to select men of their own age[17] and noted more specifically that the young Lorenzo de'Medici and the young Maximilian chose men young like themselves and consequently were "poorly advised."[18] James VI warned his son against dismissing his father's advisers.[19] Metternich noted that the young Emperor Alexander of Russia, "impulsive, always in danger of

---

[15]2 Chronicles 10:8. Generally, the Old Testament reflects the conviction that "with the ancient is wisdom; and in length of days understanding" (Job 12:12), but there is in both the Old and New Testaments another strain that finds wisdom in the poor, the young, and the innocent.

[16]*The King's Mirror*, p. 197.

[17]Commynes, p. 105.

[18]Ibid., pp. 377 and 395.

[19]James VI, *Basilicon Doron*, vol. 1, p. 111.

acting rashly" had surrounded himself with a council of persons of his own age.[20]

Those who were disposed to have reservations about "the boyish Kennedy" were not comforted by his selection of an aide and adviser who was even considerably younger than himself.[21] When the economist Paul Samuelson praised Robert V. Roosa very highly to President-elect Kennedy, the latter said, "Well if this fellow is so good, why don't we give him the top job [secretary of the treasury]?" "You can't do that," Samuelson said. "He is too young." Kennedy, who noted that Roosa was only a year younger than himself, was considerably entertained.[22] In the search for Bureau of the Budget leadership, Kennedy's Cambridge advisers were very enthusiastic about David Bell, but because of his youth "had only dared suggest him as associate director."[23]

Independent of the succession problem, youth is held to have qualities that unfit it for politics, and age to have precisely those qualities that are required. Although this judgment is not universally held, the virtues of age and the deficiencies of youth for political and particularly advisory functions have been emphasized in almost all ages and cultures. In Plato's *Laws*, the Athenian stranger states that there is no impropriety in criticizing the laws since no young men are present.[24] Aristotle thought that nature's order that endows young men with strength and old men with wisdom should be followed; the young should be warriors and only in later years counselors.[25] Wisdom, Plutarch believed, was produced by nature in old age only after a long effort, and he wrote his essay "Whether an Old Man Should Engage in Public Affairs" to protest the withdrawal of the aged from active political and even

---

[20]Metternich, vol. 1, p. 55.

[21]When John F. Kennedy became a senator, he was thirty-five years of age, and Theodore C. Sorensen was twenty-four. Sorensen tells us that he was so sensitive about his own youthfulness that he managed to keep his age secret from Senator Kennedy for two years. Sorensen, 1965, p. 17. When Kennedy was elected president, he was forty-three years old and Sorensen thirty-two. Kennedy's age was a major campaign issue, and Sorensen prepared a "youth and age" file that Kennedy used when he was given TV rebuttal time on this issue. Ibid., p. 152.

[22]Schlesinger, 1965, p. 154.

[23]Ibid., p. 137.

[24]Plato, *Laws*, bk. I(635).

[25]Aristotle, *Politics*, bk. VII, 1329^a.

military service. "The state which always discards the old men must necessarily be filled up with young men who are thirsty for reputation and power, but do not possess a statesmanlike mind."[26]

Like so many councils, the Roman senate was a council of elders. In debates in the college of augurs, age had precedence over even the very highest officers of the republic. Cicero drew attention to what he held to be an important virtue of the aged, particularly important in an adviser: they are more spirited and courageous than youth; and illustrated his point with the story of Solon, who when the tyrant Pisistratus demanded "Pray, what do you rely upon in opposing me so boldly?" replied, "Old age."[27] The prince of Ts'in was in full agreement with Cicero. The young men whom he made into his *hommes de confiance* turned out badly, and he returned to his old counselors who were not afraid of him and did not comply with his every wish.[28]

Ancient Indian tradition also shows a predilection for the aged counselor, and it is not surprising that the counselor whose wisdom saves the Crows in *The Panchatantra* is "an ancient, far-sighted counselor of his race."[29]

The European Mirrors of Kings of the Middle Ages almost uniformly advised the prince to draw his advisers from among older men of long experience whose prudence and maturity compensate for the impetuousness of the prince's youth. The young may be sincere but they are generally too bold.

This sentiment continued into the Renaissance, and Leonardo da Vinci summed it up in the harsh statement, "Let him expect disaster who shapes his course on a young man's counsel."[30] Charles V warned his son to avoid the counsels of youth and suggested that he select some old men and others of "reasonable age."[31] Nonetheless, the writers of the Renaissance show an increasing disposition to find some merit in youth or at least to warn against some of the dangers of the old. Grimaldus was firm in his belief that old men, as a result of long experience, acquire "a third

---

[26]Plutarch, *Moralia*, vol. X, pp. 113 and 115.
[27]Cicero, *De Senectute*, pp. 83–84.
[28]Couvreur, p. 397.
[29]*The Panchatantra*, p. 301.
[30]da Vinci, p. 91.
[31]Laiglesia, pp. 70–71, and 75.

eye wherewith they easily discerne the beginning . . . of things," but acknowledged that many men are already old at thirty years and have acquired prudence and wisdom. Grimaldus believed it was good practice at council meetings for the oldest members to speak first, not because the aged should be so honored, as Cicero thought, but in order to give the youngest more time to reflect.[32]

A Persian *Mirror for Princes* asserts that youth thinks itself superior to its elders and that the prince's vizier should be old and in any case not a youth. Nonetheless, this work, like that of Grimaldus, acknowledged that a person though young may be old in understanding and goes further in warning the young prince not to consort "with old fools." Indeed, "clever young men" are much to be preferred.[33]

Commynes showed little disposition to find merit in youth—the young undertake foolish enterprises and disdain counsel;[34] but Machiavelli, writing less than a generation later, took a considerably less irritable view of youth. Young men of merit should be employed in political capacities, since fortune favors youth, presumably because youth is more energetic in seizing fortune by the forelock but also because *Fortuna* is a woman.

Francis Bacon, too, had a sympathetic attitude toward youth and showed the same judiciousness and lack of prejudice that mark so many of his discussions on the art of politics. He agreed with the prevailing view that foreign missions and negotiations should not be put in the hands of a young man "not weighed in state matters." But his sympathy for the young led him to add that some young gentlemen should accompany the negotiators that they "might be thereby prepared and fitted for the like employment." Further, young men should be sent abroad to learn languages and be prepared for public employment, and thus enable the country "to breed up a nursery of such public plants."[35] In a striking essay, "Of Youth and Age," Bacon points out that "a man that is young in years may be old in hours, if he have lost no time."[36] Unfor-

---

[32]Grimaldus, pp. 94–95. Laurentius Grimaldus wrote his book *The Counsellor* in Latin "consecrated to the honour of the Polonian Empyre." It was translated into English and published in London in 1598.

[33]Ibn Iskandar, pp. 2, 34, 49, 51, and 223.

[34]Commynes, p. 282.

[35]Bacon, "Advice to Sir George Villiers," *Works*, vol. 2, p. 382.

[36]Bacon, "Of Youth and Age," *Selected Writings*, p. 110–111.

tunately, this rarely happens. He condemns the impetuousness of young men but finds that they have other virtues. "Young men are fitter to invent than to judge; fitter for execution than for counsel; and fitter for new projects than for settled business." Bacon is quite ready to acknowledge the limitations of age in positions of power. "Men of age object too much, consult too long, adventure too little, repent too soon, and seldom drive business home to the full period, but content themselves with a mediocrity of success." He concludes, naturally enough, that the virtues of each age should be employed to correct the defects of the other.

Over two thousand years ago, Aristotle had already observed that youths do extremely well in mathematics but that young men of practical wisdom are difficult to find. Mathematics deals with universals and abstractions that do not require the prolonged contact with a large variety of particulars that only a lengthy experience can give.[37] Today, when social and physical research requiring high levels of specialized training and mathematical and numerical literacy play a large role in both intellectual life and in debates on public affairs, youth's deficiencies of experience will be less disadvantageous or, at least, not so readily acknowledged to be so. The rapidity of scientific and technical development provides particular advantages to those most recently trained, and young men skilled in various technical and scientific fields have become important counselors not only in these areas but through them in many broader areas of public policy.

Engineers and Intellectuals

The old, established professions—the clergy, law, medicine, and the military—provided leadership in areas well beyond their own area of expertise. The engineer, however, despite his important role from earliest times in great civil and military undertakings has rarely made his professional status a platform for advancement to high political office. The traditional professions are skilled in the handling of people, but the skills of the engineer are in manipulating the physical world. Perhaps inclinations, dispositions, and experiences associated with this difference partly account for the limited

[37]Aristotle, *Nichomachean Ethics*, bk. VI, 1142[a].

political role of men like Archimedes and da Vinci.[38] In any event, the men who designed and built the pyramids, the ancient Chinese irrigation systems, the Great Wall of China, the Roman aqueducts and roads, and the medieval cathedrals did not achieve political fame corresponding to the character of their achievements.[39] With the exception of the Politburo since the mid-sixties, engineering triumphs in the modern world have not been accompanied by the political leadership of engineers. The presidency of Herbert Hoover only reminds us how rarely engineers have in the West achieved high political office.[40]

Although engineering skills were primarily rewarded with political advancement when associated with military undertakings, new skills applicable to day-to-day administration provided opportunities for political advancement to new groups of experts. Illustrative of these developments is the rise to power of Jean Baptiste Colbert who, as Louis XIV's Controller-General of Finance and holder of two other secretaryships of state, became Louis' principal minister after the death of Cardinal Mazarin. "Monsieur Colbert was a Merchant and an excellent Accomptant. . . . Cardinal Mezarin found that his Stables were very chardgeable to him, and was imposed upon in his Accompts. He hearing of this merchant Colbert to be a great master in this Art, sends for him and desires him to make inspection into his accounts and putt him into a better method to avoyd being abused. Which he did, and that so well that he imployed him in ordering the accounts of all his Estate and found him so usefull that he also made use of him to methodize and settle the Accompts of the King. This was his Rise."[41]

In the sixteenth century, scholars—humanists and others—began

[38]On the political significance of different professional skills, see Lasswell, 1936, pp. 130–133.

[39]Roman admiration for technical achievement was nonetheless considerable. The Romans paid greater homage to Archimedes, despite the injury his ingenuity inflicted on them, than did his native land. The Emperor Vespasian declined to employ a mechanical device invented by a Roman engineer for hauling huge columns up to the Capitol because "I must always ensure," he said, "that the working classes earn enough money to buy themselves food." Nonetheless, he gave the engineer a handsome reward. Suetonius, *Vespasian*.

[40]Perhaps one should include here the onetime military engineer and businessman President Jimmy Carter.

[41]Aubrey's *Lives*, p. 69.

to achieve a fame and a corresponding political importance that generally had been reserved for churchmen and jurists. Sir Thomas More and Erasmus are only the outstanding examples of a class of men who found themselves courted by rulers and sometimes thrust into offices for which they had little taste.

There was little disposition to show a similar respect for scientists who in Elizabethan and Stuart political life did not achieve the influence accorded letters. Nor, a hundred years later, was Swift's satire, the Academy of Lagado, an encouraging sign for their political advancement. Not even military exigencies served to breach this barrier. Poli, the celebrated Italian chemist, brought to France his invention of a poison gas and demonstrated its military potential on a flock of sheep. The success of this experiment was brought to the attention of Louis XIV who said, "This is abominable. This man must be locked up." Only the intervention of his French sponsors enabled Poli, by burning his secret, to exchange this fate for membership in the French Academy.[42]

During World War I, economists and statisticians entered government service on a substantial scale in many countries and the esteem for expert economic services generated by this wartime experience greatly increased postwar demands for contributions to practical problems.[43] The extraordinary impetus given to certain forms of pure and applied science by World War II ushered in a new era in which scientists became close advisers of political leaders, sometimes in areas only remotely related to their field of expertise. Frederick Lindemann, later Lord Cherwell, holder of the chair of physics at Oxford, a longtime friend of Winston Churchill, became, when war arrived, Churchill's personal adviser "thus in-

---

[42]Montesquieu, *Un carnet inédit* . . . pp. 231–232. Under Louis XV a certain Dupré invented a fire (presumably a reinvention of "Greek fire") "so rapid and all devouring that even water could not extinguish it." Experiments in the Versailles canal "made everyone shudder." But the king forbade use of it and paid Dupré to keep silent about his discovery. A few years later, in 1779, the French minister of the navy rejected an invention of a hollow cannonball that had the double power to penetrate enemy ships and set fire to them. The minister noted that several new inventions had been proposed to the English as well, but added that "there are no grounds for thinking that they would make use of these inventions that cannot be adopted by civilized nations." *Chronique de Versailles*, No. 802, September 20, 1945.

[43]"The Development of Social Thought and Institutions: War and Reorientation," *Encyclopedia of the Social Sciences*, vol. 1, p. 211.

augurating for him an extraordinary period of power without responsibility, power greater than that exercised by any scientist in history."[44] Although regarded as the prime minister's scientific adviser, he advised as well on economic and other problems, especially if they lent themselves to a quantitative or analytical approach.

Operations research (in England, operational research) and the development of nuclear weapons and nuclear energy marked the large-scale introduction of scientific personnel into high government levels, although World War I was not without some parallel instances. To operations research should go part of the credit for accelerating both research on policy problems and the organization and methodology of the policy sciences.[45]

The depression of 1929 had led, after the election of Roosevelt, to the New Deal in which many intellectuals and academic personalities entered government service. This entry of intellectuals into government was, however, not so striking as that which occurred in the brief Kennedy years. Intellectuals both outside and inside academic life were not so concerned as their New Deal forebears had been to redress injustices as they were to apply ideas, knowledge, and techniques often unknown to or neglected by political leaders.[46] Kennedy appointed a higher proportion of academic persons, including fifteen Rhodes scholars, to important posts than any other president. However, most of these academicians had had earlier government experience.[47] Of Kennedy's first two hundred top appointments, nearly half came from government service and politics, 18 percent from universities and foundations, and 6 percent from the business world. Eisenhower, on the other hand, had appointed 42 percent from business and 6 percent from universities and foundations.[48] A surprisingly large number of Kennedy appointees had written books, and Sorenson records a curious statistic to the effect that Kennedy's appointees "had among them written more books than the president could

---

[44]Birkenhead, p. 220.

[45]The term 'policy sciences' dates from the years following World War II. See Lerner and Lasswell, 1951; and Lasswell, 1968.

[46]Schlesinger, 1965, p. 210.

[47]Sorensen, 1965, p. 256.

[48]Seymour E. Harris, p. 25.

read in a four-year term, even at twelve hundred words per minute."[49]

The appointment of the intellectual or more generally of the expert to government office has not always gone unchallenged nor has he always been accepted with good grace. Plato had already established one theme damaging to the claims of experts, namely, that politics could not be taught and fell within the competence of every citizen. This view had difficulty surviving the complex problems of the larger modern polities. Nonetheless, the claim of experts to superior judgment was almost inevitably resented by laymen. Already in the seventeenth century, Molière could complain: "And even when it comes to eating and drinking, we no longer dare to judge what is good without the permission of these gentlemen, the experts."[50] Swift's Grand Academy of Lagado showed a similar distaste for the claims of expertise.

Political moods often produce periods in which a reaction sets in to what is believed to be the arrogance of intellectuals. The terms "McCarthyism" and "egghead" recall such periods. Recent years with their disillusionments in the political and economic spheres and the development of a whole host of troublesome domestic problems also seem to have undermined the confidence of the American public in scientists as well as other groups.[51]

Women

The image of the political adviser is that of a man. Great queens are no rarity in history, but they have no more shown a predilection for women advisers than their male counterparts. Obviously, this does not mean that women have played only a trivial role at the courts of rulers, but their role has not generally been exclusively that of a minister or official adviser. Joan of Arc is one of the few women whose name stands out as the adviser and guide to a king. In contemporary times Marcia Williams (Lady Falkender) stands

[49]Sorensen, 1965, p. 256.

[50]Molière, *La Critique de l'École des Femmes,* scene 6.

[51]According to a Louis Harris poll of 1972, "great confidence in science" declined from 56 percent in 1966 to 37 percent in 1972.

out as a close and powerful adviser to a major political leader, Prime Minister Harold Wilson.[52] Nonetheless, while filling other roles, women have also played the part of advisers and counselors. Roman writers attached considerable importance to the wife of the prince, and this emphasis was carried over into the Christian Mirrors of Kings.[53] Julian the Apostate, speaking of the prince, had said, "His wife should be good, wise, and prudent, so that she may partake of his plans and counsel him."[54] Echoing this sentiment, Aegidius Romanus, a pupil of Thomas Aquinas and completer of his work on the prince, recommended that the wife of the prince share his secrets and help him with advice.[55] Many of the authors of the Mirrors of Princes were more reserved in their judgments and restricted the wife of the prince to sharing in the education of the children. Not many wives of rulers achieved the fame and power of Justinian's Theodora or of Perón's Evita, but at lesser levels of fame their names could readily be multiplied. The great influence that Victoria, the English wife of Frederick William, heir of William I, had on her husband[56] might have had important consequences for the history of Europe had Frederick William not died almost immediately after succeeding to the throne, to be followed by William II. In the modern period, Madam Sun Yat-sen, Madam Chiang Kai-shek, Chiang Ching (Mao Tse-tung's wife), Evita Perón, and María Estela Martínez ("Isabel") de Perón illustrate wives of political leaders who have played a very substantial role of their own.

The political role played by wives of rulers is often interpreted not as counsel but as intrigue and influence. This is also true of queen mothers during both the minority of their sons and after they have reached their majority. 'Intrigue' and 'influence' rather than 'counsel' often dominate discussions of the mistresses of rulers such as Madame de Pompadour, Louis XV's *maîtresse en titre*.

---

[52]For a not entirely dispassionate account, see Haines, *The Politics of Power*.
[53]Born, 1928a, p. 503.
[54]Ibid., 1965, p. 88.
[55]Ibid., 1928a, p. 489.
[56]Holstein, vol. 1, p. 139.

Intrigue revolving around women is a stock image of Asian courts. "The intelligent ruler," wrote Han Fei Tzu, "as regards women, may enjoy their beauty but ought not to follow their entreaties and comply with their requests."[57] The subsequent history of China suggests a considerable disregard of Han Fei Tzu's advice. A Turkish opinion is more damaging to women. A vizier recommended to his ruler that he should not take counsel of women, quoting the words attributed to the Messenger, "Consult them and do the contrary."[58]

The contemporary period has seen women heads of government in India, Ceylon, Israel, and Argentina, but there have been no notable women political advisers to them. It appears that women more readily achieve the highest political position, whether as queens or heads of republican governments, than they do secondary roles, except in those cases where their secondary roles derive from their position as wives or mistresses of political leaders. Women readily achieve cabinet rank these days, but few have become politically powerful, although Margaret Thatcher, head of Britain's Conservative Party, is a clear exception. Mrs. Anne Armstrong, onetime presidential counselor with Cabinet rank and United States ambassador to Great Britian, was rumored in 1976 to be a vice-presidential prospect.

Most of the women who have played a prominent political role in the contemporary world either as heads of government or as wives or daughters of political leaders have done so in those countries where women are often thought to be especially confined to their 'traditional' roles. Indeed, even in 'traditional' preliterate societies, women have sometimes participated in councils to a degree rarely to be found in modern 'nontraditional' societies. Thus, among the Iroquois, a society organized for military action, women participated in councils and possessed a veto power over declarations of war. Their voices were also prominent in arrangements for the restoration of peace.[59]

---

[57]Han Fei Tzu, vol. 1, p. 66.
[58]*History of the Forty Vezirs*, p. 378.
[59]Landtman, p. 17

The Wandering Scholars

One might suppose that the political adviser, standing close to the center of state power, would necessarily be a national, whether naturalized or native, of the state he serves. In fact this has not been the case in many places and at many times. Our appreciation of 'one world,' of the ease and speed of travel today, and on the other hand, of the difficulty of travel in earlier ages and the immobility and immobilism of agricultural societies, has given us an exaggerated idea of our mobility relative to that of other societies and times. We may overlook, for instance, the enormous movement of poets, scholars, churchmen, doctors, jurists, and craftsmen in the Middle Ages, a movement partly inspired by the turbulence of the times but also motivated and rendered feasible by a common Christian culture and Latin language, and by the fact that these mobile sectors of the population carried their capital with them in their heads and in their hands. The fragmentation of society into the domains of feudal lords, dukes, princes, and city-states greatly multiplied the number of centers able to act as magnets for their talents.

This type of mobility, common to many early societies, had two important political consequences. It provided habituation to and tolerance for the stranger in the society, and this, in its turn, made it possible for the specialist in politics or government to find employment in lands other than that of his birth with little more resistance than might be encountered by a wandering poet, scholar, churchman or doctor.

The Greek states provided through their language, cultural uniformities, and proximity a setting in which a political expert or rhetorician could find service in a state other than his own. Greek practice of driving political enemies into exile was, as Plutarch noted, damaging to the fortunes of countries who thus supplied political talent to their potential enemies.[60] The movement of purveyors of wisdom from state to state is attested to by Plato's and Aristotle's disapproval of it. Plato thought that this wandering from

---

[60]Plutarch, *Lives*, Alcibiades and Coriolanus.

city to city unfitted the Sophists as statesmen, although later observers noted a certain advantage deriving precisely from this political cosmopolitanism.[61] Aristotle noted that one mark of the tyrant is that he prefers foreigners to citizens since the latter are likely to be his enemies but the foreigners are not rivals with him.[62] In Rome, Tacitus refers to outstanding speakers as often having a host of clients "even among foreign nations."[63]

In ancient China the common word "to wander" or "to travel" had, in Confucian circles, the technical meaning "to go from Court to Court as a peripatetic counsellor."[64] Lord Shang and Han Fei Tzu were prominent examples of this class. This did not discourage Han Fei Tzu from warning rulers not to give foreigners who had property and families abroad seats in the state council;[65] nor from calling advisers and ministers living in exile "roaming calamities" since they are able to aid neighboring enemies.[66] Ambassadors sent to negotiate with a ruler were not beyond selling their services to him.[67] As in the case of the Greek Sophists, the Chinese peripatetic persuaders and political advisers operated among states with a common written language and culture. Besides, the tradition that the Chinese Warring States all owed loyalty to a common emperor mitigated to some extent the apparent disloyalties of the peripatetic counselor.

Both Christian and Islamic society in the Middle Ages also produced professional wandering political experts. Patriotism in the modern sense was a weakly developed sentiment, and Ibn Iskandar pointed out to his son that while traveling in foreign lands he may find opportunities awaiting him: "Then cherish no longings for your own place but settle yourself where your interests lie, recognizing that place as your fatherland and as the country in which your profit lies. Although the saying goes that one's homeland is a second mother, do not be overconcerned with that."[68] Ibn Khal-

[61]Plato, *Timaeus* (19).
[62]Aristotle, *Politics*, bk. V, 1314^{a}.
[63]Tacitus, *Dialogue on Oratory*, p. 764.
[64]Waley, p. 60.
[65]Han Fei Tzu, vol. 1, p. 136.
[66]Ibid., vol. 2, p. 264.
[67]Crump, 1964, p. 8.
[68]Ibn Iskandar, p. 54.

dun had no hesitation, nor need he have had any, given the political climate of the time, in making his services available to a variety of rulers in North Africa and Spain. Nonetheless, like the wandering Sophists and the peripatetic Chinese, who remained within their own cultural orbit, Ibn Khaldun's political skills were offered only to Moslem polities. When the Christian king of Castile offered to take him into his service, Ibn Khaldun declined.

The absence of local patriotism combined with loyalty to a larger cultural or religious society that we have noted in the Chinese and Moslem case, was not so consistently observed in Christian Europe.[69] El Cid, Rodrigo Díaz of Bivar, who in the poem *El Cid* appeared as the very paragon of all the virtues of feudal Spanish society and as the unconquerable defender of Christendom against the Moors, had, in fact, when he fell out with King Alfonso of Castile, served the Moorish king of Zaragoza, until he was later reconciled with Alfonso. Don Juan Manuel, the upholder of Christian doctrine against all paganism, did not hesitate in 1327 to join the Moorish king of Granada against his own king, Alfonso XI. Giraldus Cambrensis had parents of Welsh and Norman stock, but his sentiments were basically Welsh. This did not prevent him from serving Henry II against the Welsh and providing advice on their conquest.[70] Philippe de Commynes, the trusted adviser of Charles, Duke of Burgundy, deserted his lord to become principal adviser to Burgundy's bitterest enemy, Louis XI. 'Treason' is, perhaps, not the proper term to be employed here given the political structure of the times, but to the extent that it is applicable, it is primarily treason to a person rather than to a country. Loyalty in the Middle Ages was largely based on a personal relationship and

---

[69]Nor in classical Greece. Although the Sophists moved largely in a Grecian orbit, other elements of Greek society were not resistant to the overtures of an alien ruler. Darius developed close relations with members of the Greek aristocracies as a prelude to political penetration of Greece, giving his visitors land and titles of nobility. Hermann Bengtson, p. 156. Nonetheless, both Themistocles and Alcibiades, when they fled to the Persian court retained a loyalty to Athens, and Themistocles committed suicide when he was no longer able to resist the king's demand for assistance as his adviser in a campaign against Greece. On the other hand, he had not hesitated to help Sparta against Athens. See Plutarch, *Lives*, Themistocles, pp. 182–189; Alcibiades, p. 325.

[70]See Giraldus Cambrensis, *Description of Wales*, pp. 198–201 and *The Autobiography of Giraldus Cambrensis*.

it was not always improper for a medieval warrior to leave the field of battle as soon as *his* lord was killed.

The Italian city-states of the Renaissance provided another fertile field for the peripatetic political expert. Guicciardini served both Florence and the papal state. He observed that princes sometimes treat their ministers with little regard and should therefore not complain when they leave to serve others who treat them better and reward them more generously.[71] Machiavelli, out of office in Florence, in 1513 asked his friend Francesco Vettori, Florentine ambassador to the Holy See, to find employment for him in Rome "if not in the service of Florence at least in that of Rome and the Papacy."[72] Ten years before Machiavelli wrote these words James VI warned his son "Put never a foreigner in any principal office. . . ."[73]

The casual attitude toward offering one's services to a foreign state that marked earlier epochs is generally thought to be absent from the modern period. This, however, is not quite the case. Armand Emmanuel du Plessis, duc de Richelieu, descendant of a sister of Cardinal Richelieu, was a notable French statesman of the early nineteenth century and served as France's prime minister 1815–1818 and 1820–1821. One is, therefore, little prepared to find that he had served Russia for two decades as a soldier and administrator. In 1805 he was governor of a large province north of the Black Sea. Clausewitz, an anti-Napoleonic reformer of the Prussian army, left his emperor in 1812 to fight alongside the Russians against Napoleon, anticipating, perhaps, that Prussia would turn against her oppressor. Bernhard Ernst von Bülow, father of the Bernhard von Bülow who succeeded Bismarck, was a professional diplomat who successively served Denmark, Mecklenburg, Prussia, and finally the German Empire. Bismarck himself noted that in the Prussian foreign service foreign names were common. Because of the presumed greater fluency in French of foreigners, high positions in the Prussian civil service were often held by non-Prussians.[74] In the early nineteenth century European political society was con-

[71]Guicciardini, *Maxims*, p. 42.
[72]Machiavelli, "Choix de lettres," in *Le Prince*, p. 180.
[73]James VI, *Basilicon Doron*, vol. 1, p. 117.
[74]Bismarck, vol. I, p. 6.

scious of common cultural interests and, as Kissinger has noted, did not particularly think in Vienna of Italian opera or in Russia of German philosophy as being 'foreign.' This had consequences in the political sphere. "Thus the Russian Prime Minister, Capo d'Istria, was a Greek, the Russian ambassador in Paris, Pozzo di Borgo, was a Corsican, while Richelieu, the French Prime Minister had been governor of Odessa. Wellington gave military advice to Austria in its campaign against Murat, and in 1815 both Prussia and Austria asked Stein to serve as their ambassador with the Assembly of the Confederation."[75] In 1824, Metternich wrote to Wellington, "For a long time now Europe has had for me the quality of a fatherland."[76]

In more recent years the desertion of political personalities to serve foreign powers has generally been in the context of espionage or ideological alienation. Cases resembling those of the early nineteenth century seem to be rare. Sufficiently so that when Richard Gardiner Casey, Australian minister to Washington, resigned early in World War II to accept an office in the British cabinet under Churchill, this shift of allegiance from one sovereign state to another, even though within the British Commonwealth, was protested by the prime minister of Australia.[77]

The ubiquity of the foreign political expert is not only the result of a substantial supply of mobile experts in government seeking appointments but also, on the demand side, the product of an active recruitment of them. Although Plato, as we have noted above, was contemptuous of the statesmanlike skills of the wandering Sophists, he nonetheless acknowledged that there are, in most cities and states, "a few inspired men whose acquaintance is beyond price. . . . These are they whom . . . a well-ordered city should be ever seeking out. . . . "[78]

In ancient China, we read in the biography of Lord Shang that his decision to seek work in Ch'in was stimulated by an invitation from Ch'in's duke to the capable men throughout the country.[79]

---

[75]Kissinger, 1957, pp. 320–321.

[76]*Ibid.*, p. 321.

[77]Casey himself presumably felt that a serious issue of propriety was involved since he sought advice from Felix Frankfurter and Harry Hopkins before making his decision. Moley, p. 151.

[78]Plato, *Laws*, bk. XII(951).

[79]Lord Shang, p. 10.

Later, Lu Pu-wei of Ch'in, which had a reputation for barbarism and, as a result of the policies of Lord Shang who detested "talkers," for having little use for scholars, invited scholars from the other Chinese states to come to Ch'in and entertained them so lavishly that he was soon supporting three thousand of them.[80] Han Fei Tzu complained about rulers who "search after foreign gentlemen," dismiss their native advisers and exalt foreign residents.[81] As Li Ssu, a contemporary and onetime colleague of Han Fei Tzu said, "This . . . is the golden age of the traveling politicians." Li Ssu held in Ch'in the title of Alien Minister, a title conferred on advisers employed by Ch'in who came from another state.[82]

The ease with which foreign advisers are often accepted is perhaps related to what seems to be a widespread rule among many peoples: the powers of strangers inspire greater confidence than those of one's own people. In Australia sorcerers and prophets had a reputation in proportion to their distance from home.[83] This principle has its parallel in Jesus' saying that no man is a prophet in his own country, an aphorism illustrated in early American history by the case of Benjamin Franklin whose reputation at home derived in large part from the great esteem shown him by French society and French political leaders.

The danger that an adviser might be recruited to the service of another state seemed sufficiently grave to Grimaldus for him to recommend to his prince that none of his counselors should be permitted to travel to other countries unless he was being sent there as an ambassador or as a commander or governor in war.[84] Botero, in his advice to rulers, devoted a short section to the employment of foreigners. He noted that Giovanni Galeazzo Visconti used to say that the noblest form of commerce was to win to one's service men of excellent quality and that he did not spare any cost to draw into his employment men of every nation.[85] Botero, nonetheless, advised the prince not to admit to his counsels anyone who owed allegiance to another ruler. It is difficult for such a person

---

[80]Bodde, 1940, p. 6.
[81]Han Fei Tzu, vol. 1, p. 136.
[82]Bodde, 1938, pp. 13 and 15.
[83]Landtman, pp. 147–148.
[84]Grimaldus, p. 96.
[85]Botero, p. 160.

to give an unbiased opinion, and self-interest enters in many subtle ways into political consultations.[86]

The Russians, who had a taste for hiring foreigners for political posts, did not overlook opportunities for recruitment. When Bismarck was Prussian ambassador to St. Petersburg and was being transferred to another post, he politely remarked to the Tsar that he regretted not being able to remain longer in St. Petersburg; the Tsar promptly asked him whether he would be willing to enter the Russian service.[87]

The largest-scale utilization of foreigners for political, administrative, and military service was by the Ottoman Empire after the fall of Constantinople in 1453. In this Turkish and Moslem regime, the highest offices, with the exception of those devoted to justice and religion, were occupied by a great variety of European Christians exacted as tribute by the sultan and subjected while still young to an intensive system of reeducation and training. Almost every member of the governing group of the Ottoman Empire was born a Christian, lived as such until received by the sultan, usually between the ages of 14 and 18, became Moslem, and fought and schemed as high political officers against the states of Europe and against the Church.[88]

Two final observations on the peripatetic counselor. We noted earlier Plato's view that the wandering Sophists, having no state of their own, cannot really be politicians. An opposite point of view can be defended. The individual who moves from one society to another—the 'marginal man'—often has his wits sharpened and his knowledge broadened by the great variety of experiences that his travels provide and by his increased detachment from his own society. The heightened sensitivity of the 'marginal man' equally benefits the peripatetic political counselor or leader. Bacon saw this when in his history of Henry VII he spoke of "the fortune of an

[86]Ibid., p. 46.

[87]Bismarck, vol. I, p. 341.

[88]For an interesting account of the administrative structure of the Ottoman state that reproduces a number of contemporary documents, see Lybyer. In speaking of the large scale utilization by states of foreign personnel one should at least mention the 110,000 technical assistance personnel of all nationalities, mostly serving abroad, who in 1967 were providing technical aid to the Third World.

exiled man, which had quickened in him all seeds of observation and industry."[89]

In the Introduction we noted how freely earlier writers like the Chinese realists, Commynes, Machiavelli, Guicciardini, Bacon, and many other politically experienced advisers sought to generalize their observations and their own experiences into principles of statecraft, whereas in the nineteenth and twentieth centuries great statesmen like Metternich and Bismarck were willing to set down in memoirs, letters and autobiographies an account of their political experiences, but had little inclination to generalize from their own and others' experiences. May it not be that the mobility of advisers in earlier ages who felt themselves free to work for competing states induced in them a generalizing turn of mind that the less mobile and more nationalistically centered statesmen of a later age were unable to develop? The latter are likely to be preoccupied with the special circumstances and problems of their nations. The peripatetic counselor, on the contrary, will likely be impressed by the diversity of problems and conditions that he meets and this may induce a comparative generalizing turn of mind, stimulated too, perhaps, by the incentive that the peripatetics had to write manuals of statecraft that would increase their chances of employment.

Withdrawal

The selection, recruitment and retention of advisory personnel is greatly influenced by attitudes toward public service. High office has not always been esteemed or sought after. Indeed, personal fame and the attention of the world is sometimes viewed as a threat to personal integrity, tranquility, and moral soundness. Nowhere has this sentiment been more evident than in China. For the Taoist, to be known was to be lost. Signs of special attention such as being served before other guests indicate that the dangers of fame are upon one. "All evil comes from being too well known. Already in antiquity the sages feared fame above all else. A thousand years have passed and this precept becomes ever more true."[90] When Rabbi Baer of Mezritch, the great *maggid*, "realized that he had

---

[89]Bacon, "History of the Reign of King Henry VII," p. 363.
[90]Han Yu in Margouliès, p. 129.

become known to the world, he begged God to tell him what sin of his had brought this guilt upon him."[91] The preference for obscurity may be associated with fears, sometimes vague, sometimes more specific, of the society in which one is embedded. "We live," wrote Rivarol in a terrifying observation equally true of our own day, "in a century in which obscurity protects better than the law and reassures more than innocence can."[92]

The avoidance of fame is not always, of course, a question of the avoidance of office, but the former often leads to the latter, as the Chinese case more particularly shows. Chuang Tzu devoted a chapter of his work to the sages who refused public service, fortified in this resolution by the dangers of high office and the moral degeneracy of those with whom one must work. The proclamation of the Han Emperor Wu ordering a search for men of talent who avoid government service suggests the degree to which public service was avoided.[93]

Plato believed that state to be the best in which the rulers are most reluctant to govern. In the good state, men would be willing to serve but would not be eager to do so. In reality, Plato observed, public office is generally an object of contention.[94]

Erasmus resisted the efforts by kings and even by the emperor to get him into their service.[95] He was, however, willing to serve the public interest through his writings, which he sent to rulers and princes, from whom he readily accepted money.[96] His friend and fellow humanist, Sir Thomas More, reluctantly served Henry VIII and showed a strong distaste for public office. In More's *Utopia* Raphael, who is reproached for not entering into any king's service, replies with a catalogue of the morally degrading acts that such service requires. "I do not mean," says his friend Peter, "that you should be a slave to any king, but only that you should assist them. . . ." "The change of the word," replies Raphael, "does not alter the matter."[97]

---

[91]Buber, p. 99.
[92]Rivarol [1753–1801], p. 260.
[93]See Margouliès, "Proclamation of the Emperor Wu," p. 159.
[94]Plato, *The Republic*, bk. I (347) and bk. VII (520).
[95]Gilmore, p. 92.
[96]Born, 1965, pp. 4 and 6.
[97]Sir Thomas More, p. 7.

Those who enter public service may become discouraged and withdraw when they see that no distinction is made between men with and without merit, or see, as Han Fei Tzu complained, men being preferred for office because they are able to buy them by giving gifts to the king's courtiers. As a result, "men of merit . . . give up their careers."[98] The failure of princes to accept admonition or follow advice, especially of a moral character, was also in ancient China traditional grounds for offering one's resignation.

Kautilya reflects a lesser concern with retirement than did his Chinese counterparts. But he, too, indicates that a minister who has taken care of a prince during his minority may when the prince comes of age request relief from further worry. The minister may abandon the king, too, if the king is displeased with him. If the adviser is disgusted with ministerial life, he may retire to a forest or a place of religious sacrifice.[99]

Seneca observed that Romans commonly gave disgust with public life as a reason for their political retirement, but that in fact it was really often due to waning interest and apprehension. Vatia was considered fortunate because of his life of retirement, but Seneca attributed it not to a philosophic disdain for high public office, but rather to Vatia's fear of the emperor. "What in fact he knew was how to hide rather than how to live."[100] Fear for personal safety was indeed one of the principal motives for withdrawing from the service of the king. This insecurity was sufficient for Ibn Iskandar to warn his son that when the king acts so as to make him feel completely safe, the adviser should from that moment feel insecure. "If you are being fattened by someone, you may expect very quickly to be slaughtered by him." Indeed, it is often preferable to refuse office.[101]

Western political history is not without its own heroes who preferred loss of office or even death to service to a king whose behavior they could not condone. Some were minor and obscure figures like Walter of Chatillon, who held office in the chancery of Henry II, left the king's service after the murder of Thomas à Becket, and

[98]Han Fei Tzu, vol. 1, p. 68.
[99]Shamasastry, *Kautilya's Arthasastra*, p. 288.
[100]Seneca, pp. 111 and 106.
[101]Ibn Iskandar, p. 191.

denounced Henry II in a poem.[102] Others were more notable, like Sir Thomas More, who suffered death and achieved sainthood by a similar refusal of service to his king. These acts have a more convincing ring than Metternich's persistent self-appreciation: "I have never been afraid of failing morally. The man who enters public life has always at command a sure resource against this danger, that is—retirement."[103]

Democracies can sometimes deal as harshly with their political advisers as an arbitrary ruler. Diodotus protested the imputation of dishonesty made against advisers to the Athenian assembly which made them fear to speak.[104] The McCarthy era in the United States provides sufficient illustration for the modern period.

The motives for withdrawing and remaining in public service are both substantial, and it is not surprising that a certain ambiguity enters into the discussion even of those who, like Confucius, were ready to withdraw in moral indignation. But Confucius also said: "With me there is no inflexible 'thou shalt' or 'thou shalt not.'" It is not surprising, then, to find his principal disciple saying in the *Analects*, "It is not right to refuse to serve one's country. . . . In his desire to maintain his own personal purity he subverts one of the main principles of society. A wise man in whatever office he occupies, fulfils its proper duties, even though he is well aware that right principles have ceased to make progress."[105]

La Bruyère remarked that in his day in France it required a good deal of firmness and largeness of spirit for the nobility to refrain from accepting public appointments. Few men of leisure, he noted, are able simply to remain at home and maintain their dignity without the assistance of public service. He remarked that what the wise man needs is some better word than "unoccupied" for those engaged in meditating, conversing, reading, and being tranquil. He suggested that this be called "working."[106]

A similar ambivalence toward public service exists today. Nonetheless, despite a not very high esteem for political life, United

[102]Whicher, p. 127.
[103]Metternich, vol. 1, p. 38.
[104]Thucydides, p. 168.
[105]Confucius, *Analects*, bk. 18, chaps. 7 and 8.
[106]La Bruyère, p. 50.

States presidents do not seem to have serious difficulty in enlisting the services of nonpolitical personnel. Task forces organized to advise President-elect Kennedy were manned without difficulty. Both Sorensen and Schlesinger in discussing the period preceding Kennedy's inauguration report the readiness of most academics and others to respond to invitations, recognized as carrying with them a large measure of prestige.[107] It has sometimes been supposed that John F. Kennedy had a special attraction to academic liberals, but in 1965, President Johnson established a series of task forces that also had a high rate of acceptances "especially among academics." Only 3 or 4 out of some 250 academics turned down his invitations.[108] In the early days of Kennedy's presidency, "The pleasures of power, so long untasted, were now being happily devoured—the chauffer-driven limousines, the special telephones, the top secret documents, the personal aides, the meetings in the Cabinet Room, the calls from the President."[109] A study of scientists acting as advisers and consultants in Washington reports, "All candidly state that prestige has been the strongest motivation for accepting such undertakings. They admit to the feelings of power, status, and pride these endeavors generate."[110] More recently, however, Henry Kissinger has noted that intellectuals now "volunteer less and participate less."[111] If this is so, perhaps a comment of Cicero's is applicable today. Cicero spoke bitterly of those who generally avoid public service and only offer themselves at critical moments although they have done nothing to prepare themselves for political life. "It has always seemed especially strange to me in the discourses of the learned, that men who admit that they cannot pilot the ship when the sea is calm, because they have never learned how nor troubled about such knowledge, nevertheless declare that they will take the helm when the waves are highest."[112]

---

[107]Sorenson, 1965, p. 237; Schlesinger, 1965, pp. 210–213.
[108]Thomas and Wolman, p. 133.
[109]Schlesinger, 1965, p. 213.
[110]Eiduson, p. 28.
[111]Kissinger, 1974, p. 642.
[112]Cicero, *Commonwealth*, pp. 110–111.

4

The Adviser and the Political Leader

Access

The advisory relation is decisively affected by the nature of the access that the adviser has to his principal. There are several dimensions of access that are important here. Access may be through the spoken or written word or both. In either case it may be brief or long. It may be continuous or sporadic. It may be direct or through intermediaries. It may be initiated by the leader or by the adviser. An adviser may be the principal or predominant source of advice or, on the contrary, have to compete with advice pouring in from a large number of counselors, analysts, and agencies.

Opportunities to be an educator of the ruler (see pp. 49–54) and not only an adviser on specific issues will depend on where in the spectrum the adviser is situated with respect to each of these dimensions of access. These variations in access also affect almost all other aspects of the adviser-advisee relation, and more especially the strength of the adviser's influence and the likelihood that his advice will be implemented.

Today only a few privileged advisers have the direct and continuous access of a personal counselor living as a member of his principal's household in the manner of a Patronio or a Joinville. Few have such continuous and direct relations with their principal as did Cardinal Richelieu with Louis XIII after 1626. And yet even Richelieu could complain that "the four square feet of the King's cabinet are more difficult to conquer than all the battlefields of Europe."[1] Commynes proudly affirmed that from the time when he first entered the service of Louis XI until the hour of the latter's death, he lived with the king for a longer time than any other person.[2] The 'live-in' adviser is rare in modern times, but Harry Hopkins arrived for dinner at the White House on May 10, 1940 and stayed for three and a half years, living in Lincoln's study. He was thus able, after breakfast in the morning or dinner in the evening and at odd times during the day, to talk with President Roosevelt, a degree of access that greatly enhances the influence and prestige of an adviser.

Similar to the Roosevelt-Hopkins arrangement was the provision of rooms for Frederick Lindemann (Lord Cherwell) at Number 11 Downing Street that permitted Winston Churchill in the small hours of the night to summon his adviser who had merely to walk through one of the communicating doors to Number 10.[3] These instances of almost medieval or Renaissance propinquity of ruler and adviser reflected close personal relations.

The relative lack of protocol and ritual surrounding the United States president—although he is head of state as well as head of government—has permitted, where this was congenial to the parties, a substantial intimacy between him and his advisers. Most advisers have indicated with some satisfaction in their memoirs the frequency with which they shared presidential summer homes, boating trips, planes, cars, and leisure moments. Colonel House was frequently an overnight guest at the White House and sometimes a host to the president.

Intimacy and frequency of contact are affected by the degree to which the advisory process is institutionalized or informal. Presi-

---

[1]Cited by Méthivier, p. 46.

[2]Commynes, p. 57.

[3]Birkenhead, p. 296.

dent Eisenhower's reliance on staff and cabinet meetings, and the pyramid structure of the White House staff with its various official posts that multiplied paper work, interposed barriers between the president and his responsible officers and advisers. President Kennedy abolished these practices and made himself more accessible through informal meetings and direct contact with individual staff members. He talked both at the White House and by telephone with subordinate government experts, although independently of this, they, of course, did not have access to him. His initiatives in this respect were motivated, in part, by a fear that he might be cut off in the White House from useful counsel or criticism.[4]

Failure to provide access runs the risk so well noted by Gracián and so well illustrated by President Nixon: "There are some that are incorrigible simply because they are inaccessible: they fall to ruin because none dares to extricate them."[5] Isolation is sometimes due not to a desire to remain inaccessible but to a powerful adviser or official who is able to protect what he conceives to be either his own or his principal's interest by blocking access to him. Richelieu remarked that it is dangerous to allow access to the king to "persons of ill intent" since the king is likely to be impressed more by the number of complainants than the solidity of their complaints.[6] Frederick Lindemann operated to maintain a monopoly, and his scientific rivals found it virtually impossible to get an independent hearing by Churchill. These situations are only removed in degree from those encountered in Eastern courts. At the Ottoman court the Kizlar Aga or the Chief Black Eunuch, principal ministrant to his master's personal pleasures, controlled all communications between the sultan and his ministers. Not even the grand vizier could ignore him.[7]

Exclusive and intimate working relations need not always depend on frequent or continuous face-to-face contact. The collaboration of Louis XVIII and his young minister Élie Decazes was mediated through the *portefeuille itinérant* brought by Decazes to Louis every morning with Decazes' memos and comments, and picked up again

---

[4]Sorensen, 1965, p. 281–282.
[5]Gracián, p. 87.
[6]Richelieu, *Maximes d'état . . .* , Maxim CXLV.
[7]Cassels, p. 55.

each evening by him with Louis' replies, memos, and marginal commentaries. Decazes and Louis were the sole possessors of the two keys that locked and unlocked the *portefeuille itinérant*.[8]

A principal barrier restricting access to the ruler is the limited amount of time he disposes of and has available for his advisers. It is precisely this that gives special value to continuous, intimate relations of an adviser with his principal, for this intimacy generally assures a privileged portion of the ruler's time. Today many policy analysts or advisers deal with a limited area or issue on which they claim special competence. Since numerous other advisers in this same specialty are making their voices heard, and since a great number of other matters also clamor for the attention of the leader, the contemporary policy analyst is taught, in addressing himself to high levels, to reduce his findings or his advice to a single page or at the most to five pages. If the analyst is to have direct access to his principal, he is carefully rehearsed by briefing experts so that the greatest effect may be squeezed from the ten or fifteen minutes allotted to the briefing. Under such circumstances the policy adviser is, to say the least, hardly likely to be much of an educator and his advice even on a specific issue is likely to be confined to the barest skeleton of a coherent argument. It was the preciousness of time that made Lindemann so great an asset to Winston Churchill. Churchill demanded the utmost brevity in communications, and Lindemann had a talent for reducing documents to their bare essentials and providing the result to Churchill in a manner that permitted easy absorption, especially in the case of statistical materials not easily understood by Churchill.

The great majority of persons and institutions capable of providing counsel and assistance to a political leader must almost necessarily do so through the written word. Given the amount of material that flows across the desk of a political leader (and his top advisers) it is apparent that accessibility through the written word will depend on how accustomed he is to read, how comfortable he feels with written material, and whether or not he needs everything predigested for him into a *précis* of a *précis*. Machiavelli was

[8]The warmth of Louis' feelings for Decazes is indicated by the abbreviations he invented to address Decazes: "m.c.e." (mon cher enfant); "t.p.t.L. (ton père, ton Louis). Langeron, p. 65.

able to assume that the hundred pages of his *Prince* would not impose too great a burden on Lorenzo de' Medici's time, although he was sufficiently sensitive to the competition for the time of a prince to emphasize in his second paragraph that the book was brief enough to enable Lorenzo to master "in a very short time" all that he needed to know concerning the art of government. Machiavelli was, presumably, less interested in the influence he could exercise through the *Prince,* than in the opportunity—never realized—that the book might afford a personal post with Lorenzo. In Machiavelli's day, as in earlier centuries, the written word whether as a treatise, a simple memorandum, or a formal memorial to the throne was often intended as a prelude to or an accompaniment of personal access to the leader. The enormous literary influence of Machiavelli's *Prince* in the century after it was written was probably not what its author aspired to in writing it.

Unfortunate indeed is the adviser whose principal does not like to read or is incapable of rapidly digesting documents and reports. Von Bülow noted this difficulty with William II who disliked having to read even the shortest *comptes rendus*.[9] General Eisenhower was said not to be much of a reader except for the Western novels of Zane Grey. Truman, by contrast, had been an avid reader since boyhood and Dean Acheson noted that "It was never necessary to *digest* anything for him, to simplify. . . . Mr. Truman read the documents themselves, and he understood and acted on them."[10] President Truman himself, speaking of the papers that piled up on his desk, wrote: "I have always been a heavy reader, and it is easy for me to concentrate. Fortunately, too, my memory is retentive. . . ."[11] Metternich, too, could absorb large amounts of written materials and maintained an intensive correspondence with his ambassadors abroad.[12]

The limited access of the contemporary policy analyst to his principal has one perhaps unexpected consequence of great interest. The principal generally being a literate person will find occasion, perhaps while traveling or perhaps during an evening away

---

[9]von Bülow, vol. 3, p. 132.
[10]Cited in Miller, p. 52.
[11]Truman, vol. 1, p. 26.
[12]Sauvigny, p. 100.

from his office, to consume a certain amount of literature. It may thus happen that he will take the time to read a twenty-page article in, say, *Foreign Affairs* or even an entire book and thus accord to a writer in the public prints an amount of time and attention that it is virtually impossible for the principal's own analysts and advisers to get. Indeed, an analyst may find, in competing with outside sources of advice, that it is easier for him to get top level attention through open publication than by official studies and reports. It is not always true, then, that the 'inside' analyst has superior access to the political leader. In any event, the writer in the public media generally has a greater opportunity to *educate* by virtue of his more extended, written access to the decision maker. President Kennedy's first acquaintance with the man he chose for his secretary of state, Dean Rusk, was through an article the latter had written in *Foreign Affairs* in the spring of 1960 entitled, "The President."[13]

The press has increasingly become an important source of information for the political leader and a means for learning what information others are receiving. It is also a source of advice and admonition from many who would have no other means of access to him. President Nixon, it appears, relied on summaries and selections prepared daily in the "President's Daily News Briefing" that capsulized the editorials and stories of seventy-five newspapers, about twenty magazines and three television networks. President Ford is said to have read several newspapers a day in addition to these summaries. "Both John and Robert Kennedy gained new ideas and insights from their constant attention to the press. . . . *The New York Times* was in a sense the Kennedys' second bible, devoured each day from start to finish and credited with great influence for its news and editorial judgments. . . ."[14] Prime Minister Trudeau's statement quoted earlier (p. 14) suggests that some newspaper writers may have readier access to a political leader than his own diplomats. It is probably not possible to demonstrate in any convincing fashion the precise degree of influence exercised by the media through their access to the minds of political leaders.

---

[13]Schlesinger, 1965, p. 141.
[14]Sorenson, 1969, pp. 70–71.

Nonetheless, one must presume that they are powerful rivals of official advisers in the struggle for access.

Ordinary citizens sometimes seek access to the political leader through the one means available to them—letters and telegrams. Political leaders are generally not insensitive to political currents at the grass roots and sometimes are not indifferent to individual letters brought to their attention or to the quantity of letters received and the drift of their opinions. President McKinley used to receive about 100 letters per day, President Wilson, in 1917, 800 letters per day; President Franklin D. Roosevelt, during his first week in office, received 450,000 letters. Roosevelt worried when his mail dwindled. He did not permit replies by form letters and kept a staff occupied answering them. President Carter, after three months in office, still received 87,000 letters in one week, although this followed some stimulation by the White House to write to the President. President Eisenhower in 1952 and President Truman in 1948 received slightly more than 100 letters per year for every 10,000 literate adults in the United States, a figure that compares with a rate of 44 for Lincoln during the Civil War, of 47 for Wilson during World War I, and of 160 for Franklin D. Roosevelt during the depression and 111 in the late thirties.[15] Congressmen, too, are not insensitive to mail from their constituents, but it probably serves, as it does for the president, more as an informal referendum on current issues than as a source of advice.

Numbers

Since an adviser's access to his principal depends on how many other advisers or sources of advice the latter has, it is not surprising that the more eminent and self-confident advisers have favored a limited number of counselors. Kautilya remarks that "this kind of seeking for advice is infinite and endless. The king should consult three or four ministers. Consultation with a single minister may not lead to any definite conclusion in cases of complicated issues. A single minister proceeds willfully and without restraint. In deliberating with two ministers, the king may be overpowered by

[15]Sussmann, p. 11.

their combined action, or imperiled by their mutual dissension. But with three or four ministers he will not come to any serious grief, but will arrive at satisfactory results. With ministers more than four in number, he will come to a decision [only] after a good deal of trouble; nor will secrecy of counsel be maintained without much trouble."[16] Bacon and Richelieu, too, thought that for a strong king three or at most four counselors sufficed.[17] Almost two thousand years and half the world separate Kautilya from Richelieu but their opinions on this matter are identical. Some of this may have been self-serving; however there seems little doubt that many politically experienced men were convinced that a multiplication of advisers led to confusion. Perhaps it is significant that a principal defender of the advantage of having many counselors was not a counselor but a king. Solomon insists on three separate occasions in the *Book of Proverbs* that "in a multitude of counselors there is safety."

Charles V remarked to his son that it certainly saved a good deal of trouble to talk with only one counselor but that this was hardly to be recommended. One motive here was to avoid falling into the hands and power of a particular counselor or clique.[18] In the contemporary period this motive still operates, but an additional concern begins to play a major role, namely a fear of making a mistake and the hope that one can ensure against this by obtaining many opinions.[19] Kennedy, although he wanted his personal staff to be small, liked to get varying points of view from many advisers.[20]

Multiple advisers are only useful if they bring to their task a variety of experiences and talents and do not engage in collusion to impose a particular form of advice. Budé thought it essential that each counselor propose his own preferred solution to problems without being influenced by his colleagues.[21] For this reason the ruler is sometimes advised, as by Hobbes, to interrogate each of his advisers separately, so that he can better ensure independence of their views.[22] Franklin D. Roosevelt sometimes followed this

---

[16]Shamasastry, *Kautilya's Arthasastra*, p. 28.
[17]Richelieu, *Political Testament*, p. 61.
[18]Armstrong, p. 81.
[19]Kissinger, 1960, p. 343.
[20]Sorensen, 1965, p. 391 and Schlesinger, 1965, p. 159.
[21]Budé, p. 64.
[22]Hobbes, p. 138.

practice and often concealed from his advisers the sources of his information.[23] Kennedy, too, appreciated the advantage of independence of judgment and avoided too close coordination between his different advisers and advisory groups.[24]

Whether the advisory staff of the ruler is large or small, a question arises whether it should be organized in some hierarchical fashion or at least have a leader. Richelieu was adamant that the king's three or four advisers must have among them one who has superior authority. No doubt he was here defending his own position. A position of leadership need not require an official title or public recognition but may equally develop from an informal understanding. President Eisenhower preferred clear-cut lines of authority, and Sherman Adams was his chief of staff. The Kennedy staff members, on the contrary, were not distinguished by rank and had few differences in title, Kennedy serving as his own chief of staff.[25]

The number of advisers is likely to be proportional both to the number of different problems with which the decision maker must deal and the degree of specialized knowledge that these problems require. In the contemporary world both the variety of problems and types of specialized expertise have increased greatly. It is not surprising, therefore, that the number of advisers, boards, committees, commissions, and task forces has also grown enormously. Bacon was already fully aware in his time that the multiplicity of very different concerns on which advice was required implied an increase in the number of advisers. But to this Bacon was opposed. "Asking counsel in one business of one man, and in another business of another man" is better than nothing at all, but is dangerous. Bacon draws a parallel with the medical specialist who "may put you in a way for a present cure, but overthroweth your health in some other kind; and so cure the disease and kill the patient." He concluded that a counselor who understands the entire position of his principal will also understand with respect to any single piece of business the side effects of a particular decision. "Scattered counsels . . . will rather distract and mislead, than settle and direct."[26] Hobbes took the claims of special expertise and the division

[23]Neustadt, pp. 156–157.

[24]Schlesinger, 1965, p. 123.

[25]Sorensen, 1965, p. 262 and Schlesinger, 1965, p. 124.

[26]Bacon, "Of Friendship," *Selected Writings*, p. 74.

of labor more seriously than Bacon. "No man is presumed to be a good counsellor, but in such business, as he hath not only been much versed in, but hath also much meditated on, and considered."[27] Clearly his is the more modern view.

As the number of advisers increases, advice almost inevitably gets to be formed through debate in committees and councils, and once this process sets in a tendency toward decisions on a majority basis may occur. Hobbes was convinced that a man does best to do without any advice at all if the alternative is to depend on a council "which cannot move but by the plurality of consenting opinions. . . ." Many eyes, says Hobbes, see more than one but adds, in a striking image, that though people look with two eyes "yet they never aim but with one."[28] Bismarck felt that real responsibility required a single directing minister and not a board with majority voting.[29] Metternich shared this view.[30] Guicciardini's contempt for committee-thinking was encapsulated in the maxim that if you put eight intelligent men to consult together in a room they become so many madmen.[31] Kissinger views group or committee decision making as an unfortunate development of our times.[32]

Council or cabinet meetings do not necessarily imply the rule of majority opinion. Rulers may use meetings to encourage the shock of opinion with opinion but their own decison may have little to do with the drift of opinion in the council meeting. Even so, the use of lengthy group deliberations sometimes seems to justify Guicciardini's biting judgment. Accounts of the process by which the Cuban missile crisis was so successfully resolved convey an air of frantic, hectic, and perhaps time-wasting group deliberation in lengthy, exhausting sessions and contrast curiously with a certain air of orderly, relatively calm, purposiveness of the less group-oriented deliberations of President Truman and his advisers during the half-dozen critical decisions he made during his years in office.

---

[27]Hobbes, p. 137.
[28]Ibid., p. 139.
[29]Bismarck, vol. I, p. 308.
[30]Sauvigny, p. 46.
[31]Guicciardini, *Maxims*, p. 69.
[32]Kissinger, 1960, pp. 341–346.

Committees tend to grow too large. We already noted this in the case of the National Security Council. Many cabinets are too large for effective discussion, particularly if the cabinet members' assistants and some of the presidential advisers and press attachés also attend. The British cabinet grew from five in 1740 to fourteen in 1841, had reached a peak of twenty-three when World War II broke out, and declined to sixteen by the end of the War.[33] Even this number was thought to be awkward and a tendency developed for a smaller, inner cabinet to exercise most of the cabinet's functions. More recently, in March 1974, the French cabinet was sharply reduced in number from thirty-eight to sixteen by the exclusion of its junior ministers. Kennedy was little interested in joint deliberations of his cabinet, preferring to discuss with each cabinet member individually those matters on which he was best qualified to offer advice.[34]

Rivalry

Multiple advisers, especially without a dominant member, almost inevitably develop rivalry among themselves. Depending on the importance of the ruler and the emotions he arouses, this rivalry may become not simply a struggle for prestige, job security, and material gain, but take on the character of sibling rivalry or the rivalry of jealous suitors for a woman's favors. A Chinese tale from Hi K'ang's *Lives of the Sages* is apposite. Hai T'ang was venerated by the whole country. One day when the prince was seated with him Hai T'ang left the room. At this moment the minister Chou-haing entered. The prince stretched his legs and said, "While I was seated with Master Hai, . . . my legs became stiff but I did not dare to stretch them in his presence." Chou-haing was vexed and showed his discontent. The prince said to him, "Do you want honors? I will ennoble you. Do you want riches? I will give them to you. Master Hai has no wishes. All that I can do for him is to

[33]"Parkinson Looks at Cabinet Governments," *The Economist*, November 3, 1956, p. 396.
[34]Sorensen, 1965, p. 283.

show before him a deferential attitude. I cannot reward him otherwise. Why are you discontented?"[35]

So common is rivalry among advisers that Tacitus made a point of noting that Seneca and Burrus guided the young Nero "with a unity of purpose seldom found where authority is shared."[36] This did not prevent less favored advisers from seeking to undermine them. Those who stand outside the envied circle of intimacy are prone to keep a sharp eye on any shifts in the relationship that may foretell the decline in authority of an adviser. Bismarck's position during his early days as minister-president was rendered difficult because the age of William I suggested that Bismarck's reign might soon end. Politicians did not foresee that William I would live another twenty years.[37]

Ibn Khaldun, in an attempt to suppress the traditional rivalry of advisers, urged each, when praised, to attribute the merit to his colleagues but always to bear any blame by himself. None should boast of how much better he handled difficult affairs.[38] Budé had the same concern and urged advisers not to allow hostility against one of their colleagues to interfere with the pursuit of their common missions.[39]

Widespread failure to avoid the traditional rivalry of advisers is not surprising since, quite apart from motives arising from relations among themselves, the ruler himself has often deliberately fostered rivalrous relations. Aristotle advised the tyrant that if he raised one man to eminence, he should raise two or more others "that they may look sharply after one another."[40] Bacon, too, appreciated that "counsellors are not commonly so united, but that one counsellor keepeth sentinel over another. . . ."[41] Han Fei Tzu cautioned the ruler that a minister may attempt to undermine criticism of him by his colleagues by warning the ruler that they were jealous of

---

[35]Margouliès, p. 139. The story of Hai T'ang instructs us why in Lasswell and Kaplan (1950), p. 88, it is said, "Influence over power [based on respect] we refer to as *councilorship*."

[36]Tacitus, *The Annals*, p. 285.

[37]Holstein, vol. 1, p. 139.

[38]Ibn Khaldun, *The Muquaddimah*, vol. 2, pp. 31 and 34.

[39]Budé, p. 61.

[40]Aristotle, *Politics*, bk. V, 1315[a].

[41]Bacon, "Of Counsel," *Selected Writings*, p. 57.

him.[42] Charles V warned his son Philip to disapprove of quarrels among his ministers. At the same time, to prevent Philip from falling into the hands of one or another faction, Charles placed leaders of the two chief factions at the head of government.[43] Roosevelt is said to have enjoyed instigating bickering among his top advisers.[44] This was not particularly difficult to do given both the irascible character of Ickes and general resentment at the preference shown Hopkins. Louis M. Howe, Roosevelt's campaign manager and adviser, was "a jealous watchdog," and this required the utmost discretion in the conduct of anyone close to Roosevelt.[45]

The appointment by President Eisenhower of a United States ambassador to the United Nations instigated another form of rivalry among the president's official and unofficial advisers. Ambassador Lodge operated at the United Nations as his own secretary of state. "I am not bound by instructions from the State Department. I am a member of the President's Cabinet and accept instructions only from him." This "two-headed foreign office" continued under President Kennedy with Adlai Stevenson.[46]

The elevation of a political figure to a higher political post generally involves an expansion of his personal and advisory staff and may lead to rivalry between the original core of advisers and the new men. Theodore Sorensen, who had been with Kennedy as a senator, felt that no one knew Kennedy's mind as well as he did and, proud of his relationship with Kennedy, resented interlopers. Nonetheless, after the presidential electoral campaign was over, a measure of peace was established by a division of labor that gave Sorensen particular authority in the area of Kennedy's legislative program and domestic policy.[47] Sorensen himself has remarked: "A group of able and aggressive individualists, all dependent on one man, could not be wholly free from competitive feelings or from scornful references to each other's political or intellectual backgrounds."[48] In addition to the division of labor which insulated his

---

[42]Han Fei Tzu, vol. 1, p. 152.
[43]Armstrong, p. 80.
[44]Truman, vol. 1, p. 56.
[45]Moley, p. 135.
[46]Bailey, p. 24.
[47]Schlesinger, 1965, pp. 70 and 208.
[48]Sorensen, 1965, p. 260.

advisers to some extent from each other, President Kennedy tended to keep his relations with his aides on a bilateral basis, thus avoiding collective confrontations such as staff meetings where each aide might find out what the others were doing.[49] Whether this entirely dissipated anxiety among them is not clear, but the "ruthless scramble for access and power" that Schlesinger had anticipated did not seem to take place.

Perhaps no rivalry in modern times is so well known as that between Frederick Lindemann, Winston Churchill's scientific and general adviser, and a number of the most important scientists in the British war effort such as Tizard and Blackett. The bitter disagreements between Tizard and Lindemann are of particular interest in view of the fact that they involved areas of scientific analysis in which the role of arbitrary or personal opinion is thought to be substantially reduced. The intrigue and jealousy between these eminent scientists was all the more striking because Tizard and Lindemann had once been very close friends. Many conflicts among rival advisers continue in a more or less seesaw or indeterminate fashion, but the Tizard-Lindemann conflict was also remarkable by virtue of Lindemann's complete victory and the total crushing of his scientific opposition.[50]

The United States had its own case in the fierce dispute that raged in 1969 among scientists involved in advising government on the desirability of developing an antiballistic missile (ABM) program. The ensuing perversions of scientific judgment led to an inquiry and report by an ad hoc Committee on Professional Standards of the Operations Research Society of America.[51] This case of adviser rivalry did not, however, share several features that made the British case so dramatic—the collegial relations that had existed among the rivals and the presence of a great leader, Churchill, access to whom was at stake in the quarrel.

The rivalry among advisers is sometimes exacerbated by the distinction between those who feel themselves entitled to advise the

---

[49]Schlesinger, 1965, p. 207.

[50]Birkenhead, pp. 196–198 and 223–224 and Snow, p. 33. Both of these works need to be read in their entirety for an understanding of this famous case. See also Harrod.

[51]For the report of the Committee, see *Operations Research*, September 1971, 19(5), pp. 1123–1258. See also the issue of January-February 1972, 20(1), pp. 205–244.

ruler by virtue of custom or law and those who have a purely private advisory relationship to the ruler, that is those who have, as Hobbes would say, "no Authority of Judicature or Command, but only of giving Advice to the Sovereign when it is required. . . ."[52] The conflict between courtiers and retainers, on the one hand, and the king's advisers and ministers, on the other, constituted a somewhat similar conflict, as did the conflict of the barons or nobles with the king's advisers drawn from the clerical class.

Although personal advisers have, in theory, "no Authority of Judicature or Command," they almost inevitably acquire, through the authority they derive from the ruler, a power that has no legal or constitutional basis. Seneca and Burrus wielded enormous but unofficial authority during the early years of Nero's reign. Sir John Eliot's attack, in the early seventeenth century, on the Duke of Buckingham implied that private counselors of the king should possess the confidence of Parliament.[53] The conflict between those holding a parliamentary mandate and the unofficial advisers who depend directly on the person of the leader has continued from Eliot's day through to the struggle to divest the advisers of President Nixon of their influence and authority.

The personality and bearing of the private adviser will mitigate or exacerbate his relations with those who hold constitutional offices. Colonel House believed that President Wilson sometimes did his cabinet an injustice and failed to call on political leaders for advice as much as was desirable.[54] House's uncompetitive attitude toward President Wilson's official advisers in the early years of his relation with the President was generally rewarded by a greater tolerance by the cabinet and Congress than has been shown to other prominent presidential counselors.[55] The public sometimes ex-

---

[52]Hobbes, p. 129.

[53]Gooch, p. 65.

[54]House, vol. 1, p. 88 and vol. 2, p. 468.

[55]When House was sent to Paris in his first official position as head of the U.S. Peace Commission, his potential rivalry with the cabinet and Congress was thereby diminished but a new note of rivalry with the president himself seems to have entered into their relations. It is not clear that the change from House's unofficial to an official status was responsible, even partially, for the tension that ultimately developed between these two men. On this point, see George and George, pp. 244 and 345–346. During the final stage of House's work in Paris, it appears that

pressed puzzlement but relatively little concern about the "assistant president." However, when House undertook important and somewhat mysterious missions to Europe before and after the outbreak of war, anti-Administration newspapers raised questions concerning the president's constitutional power to appoint an "agent of high diplomacy" without Senate approval.[56]

Harry Hopkins' relations with Roosevelt's official family stand in sharp contrast with the tolerance for Colonel House and reflect both the more abrasive personality of Hopkins and the privileges of intimacy accorded him by Roosevelt. During the years he lived in the White House "he was generally regarded as a sinister figure, a backstairs intriguer, an Iowan combination of Machiavelli, Svengali and Rasputin."[57] Nor was this attitude by any means confined to professional haters of Franklin D. Roosevelt. The position of Hopkins was complicated by the fact that he oscillated between an unofficial and an official cabinet status as secretary of commerce, although his attention to that office was for much of the time casual.

Sherman Adams, both by title and the formal character of White House organization under Eisenhower, approached an official status, although the plan attributed to Eisenhower of instituting "a team of grand viziers" to be called the First Secretary and the Executive Assistant to the president was never realized.[58]

The large number of "New Frontiersmen" introduced into the administration by President Kennedy distressed State Department officials.[59] In the Nixon administration Henry Kissinger was soon judged by the world to be secretary of state in all but name, although he did not become accountable to Congress until he succeeded Secretary Rogers in this office in 1973.

Rivalry of official with unofficial members of an administration also arises from the practice of soliciting policy advice from ad hoc

---

Secretary of State Lansing resented that the meetings the president attended were held in Colonel House's suite and that House briefed the press. Edith Bolling Wilson, p. 226.

[56]House, vol. 2, pp. 112–113.

[57]Sherwood, p. 1. There were exceptions to the cabinet resentment against Hopkins' unofficial position of authority. Secretary of War Henry L. Stimson considered Hopkins' presence in the White House "a Godsend." Ibid., p. 13.

[58]Schlesinger, 1965, p. 122.

[59]Sorenson, 1965, p. 534.

committees of nongovernmental experts. Partly this practice derives from the belief that various government advisory staffs have departmental or other biases that need to be corrected by the use of outside experts.[60] Partly the unofficial advisers are used by political leaders to "prevent career men from circumventing presidential policy."[61] Partly outside experts and advisers provide, as they did for Roosevelt, another means for establishing competitive sources of information and for dividing authority among a wide range of individuals and organs.[62]

Nothing attests so well the power of rulers and the rivalry of advisers than the flattery of which the ruler is the object. There are few points on which both rulers and the writers of manuals of statecraft are more completely agreed than on this evil. Flatterers are, according to *The Panchatantra*, "Foemen in disguise."[63] Flee flatterers, Charles V told his son, "as you would the fire. They are much more dangerous."[64] James VI instructed his son to choose counselors who were "speciallie free of that filthy vice of Flattery, the pest of all Princes, and wracke of Republickes."[65]

Commynes points out that those who flatter the prince tend to exacerbate his worst faults. "If he wants to levy a penny tax, they say levy two. If he threatens a man, they say hang him. . . . They advise him above all to make himself feared. . . . They hope thereby that they themselves will be feared. . . ."[66]

Frederick the Great wrote that there was not a book on morality nor a book of history in which the weakness of princes for flattery was not fiercely reproved. To a vicious prince, flattery is a mortal poison, and with princes of merit flattery is a rust that dims the brilliance of their glory. More important, the flatterers and yesmen

---

[60]Kissinger, 1960, p. 346.
[61]Truman, vol. 2, p. 165.
[62]Neustadt, pp. 156–157.
[63]*The Panchatantra*, p. 292.
[64]Laiglesia, p. 71.
[65]James VI, *Basilicon Doron*, vol. 1, p. 115. Despite this striking phrase, James was notoriously susceptible to flattery. See Ashton, pp. 234–237 for a revealing contemporary letter instructing a would-be courtier how to exploit James I's weaknesses.
[66]Commynes, p. 351.

who surround the prince prevent him from learning the truth, and for this reason kings should be pitied and the flatterers condemned by the hatred of the public.[67] Budé stressed the same point. The prince should so behave as to encourage absolute frankness; his principal aides must have the freedom and boldness to inform him of the exact state of his kingdom.[68]

The inability to eliminate the flattery of servitors led several writers of Mirrors of Kings to recommend that the ruler rely more on books and less on persons for his instructions since the latter do and the former cannot flatter.[69] Bacon made the same point: "It was truly said, *optimi consiliarii mortui:* [the best counsellors are the dead:] books will speak plain when counsellors blanch."[70]

Callières, a French diplomat in the service of Louis XIV, pointed out that rulers have such an unbroken experience of obedience that they become sensitive to criticism, and it is by no means easy to speak the truth to them. He did not so much advise avoiding flattery entirely as developing it into a subtle art. Rulers, being accustomed to hearing their praises sung all the time, "become connoisseurs in praise and good judges of a timely compliment."[71]

The danger to the ruler arising from flattery and other forms of insincerity and, on the other hand, the necessity for the advisers to read his prince's thoughts and be warned by them, have given to both parties a need to conceal their own thoughts and penetrate those of the other. La Rochefoucauld said, "It is more difficult to conceal the sentiments that we have than to feign those that we do not have."[72] But a good deal of attention has been given, nonetheless, to penetrating the minds of others by studying their gestures, intonations, and expressions.

In India, those "who can delve into the innermost thoughts" of others and are skillful in guessing their minds were thought to make both good ministers and good spies.[73] Han Fei Tzu recom-

---

[67]Frederick the Great, *L'anti-Machiavel*, pp. 314–317. See the similar thought of William Penn, p. 13 above.

[68]Budé, pp. 60 and 134.

[69]In fact, it is quite possible for authors to flatter princes by their books, especially by fulsome dedications common in such works.

[70]Bacon, "Of Counsel," *Selected Writings*, p. 58.

[71]Callières, p. 104.

[72]La Rochefoucauld, p. 486.

[73]*Sources of Indian Tradition*, p. 255, and Shamasastry, *Kautilya's Arthasastra*, pp. 17–18.

mended that the ruler in listening to his ministers should look drunk, presumably to make them more careless in their behavior, and never to move his own lips, that is, to speak until his subordinates had done so, since their choice of words would enable him to understand their real intentions.[74]

Subtlety is not usually attributed to the Romans, but Cicero treated the problem of unmasking the minds of others better than most early writers. "We . . . may make great discoveries from very trifling circumstances. From the cast of the eye, the bending or unbending of the brow, an air of dejection or cheerfulness, laughter, the tone of words, silence, the raising or falling of the voice, and like circumstances, we may easily form a judgment which of them are in their proper state, and which of them are in discord with duty and nature."[75]

Bacon reproached Aristotle for not having realized that the gestures of the body are comprehensible. "The Motions of the countenance and parts . . . do further disclose the present humour and state of the mind and will. For as Your Majesty saith most aptly and elegantly, 'As the tongue speaketh to the ear, so the gesture speaketh to the eye.' And therefore a number of subtile persons whose eyes do dwell upon the faces and fashions of men, do well know the advantage of this observation, as being most part of their ability; neither can it be denied but that it is a great discovery of dissimulations, and a great direction in business."[76]

According to Callières, the true negotiator should be able to infer from the least movement of the countenance of his opposite number the passions that are stirring within. Even the most practiced negotiator is sometimes unable to repress these movements of his features. The negotiator should govern his conduct just as much by what he observes in the faces of others as by what he hears from their lips.[77]

The attention given to penetrating the thoughts of others is reflected in Swift's Grand Academy of Lagado whose political department contains a researcher who provides statesmen with a

---

[74]Han Fei Tzu, vol. 1, p. 56.
[75]Cicero, *Offices*, p. 70.
[76]Bacon, "Advancement of Learning," *Selected Writings*, pp. 269–270. 'Your Majesty' here refers to King James I and his *Basilicon Doron*, bk. III.
[77]Callières, pp. 19 and 121.

means to disclose the thoughts and designs of others by analyzing their excrement.[78]

The art of penetrating the minds and hearts of others was elevated at the end of the seventeenth century to the rank of a new science by Christian Thomasius, called the father of the German Enlightenment. In an essay prematurely entitled "Discovery of the Science of Learning Other People's Opinions," and presented to the Elector of Brandenburg in 1692, Thomasius promised much and delivered little, so much so that another scholar used him as an example of the charlatanism of scholars. In a later essay, Thomasius attempted to provide more substance for his new science, but the Elector of Brandenburg was hardly likely to advance his political penetration by studying it any more than by the earlier paper.[79]

We have already noted Truman's ability, said to derive from his close study of history and attested to by Dean Acheson, to penetrate the masks of other people. More recently, 'bugging' has become a more certain and less arduous method of learning the thoughts of others.

The tensions under which a ruler or political leader works often render him a touchy and sensitive person who has to be approached with great tact. Where this condition is fulfilled, an adviser may influence a ruler who is not disposed to be ruled by other people. For Louis XIV, Colbert, a bourgeois, was essentially a clerk who did his bidding, but Colbert was able to impose on Louis decisions he himself had made. Tact often requires that advice be given so as not to seem advice. You must, says Ibn Khaldun, contrive to influence the ruler in the subtlest manner.[80] For Han Fei Tzu the commonplace tricks of the sophist are not enough, since the real difficulty in addressing a ruler "consists in . . . understanding his state of mind and knowing how to adapt one's arguments to it."[81] Subtlety, tact, and indirection are particularly emphasized in classical Asian political contexts and frequent ancedotes illustrate to

---

[78]Swift, p. 226.

[79]Christian Thomasius, pp. 60–79.

[80]Ibn Khaldun, *The Muqaddimah*, vol. 2, p. 32.

[81]Waley, p. 242.

the ambitious servants of the ruler how to convey thoughts in a manner that will not excite his sensitivities. When Harun al-Rashid dreamt that all his teeth had fallen out, his dream interpreter told him that this signified that all his kinsmen would die before him. Harun ordered the interpreter beaten with a hundred blows. He called for a second interpreter who told Harun that the dream meant that he would live longer than any of his kinsmen. Harun remarked that the meaning was the same, but there was a difference in the way it was told, and gave the second interpreter a hundred dinars.[82]

It is not only fear of the ruler that motivates delicacy of communication. The tradition of not brutally imposing one's views has a wide currency in the East. When Duke Wen of Ts'in was about to attack the state of Wei, his friend Prince Tchou simply looked at the sky and smiled. The Duke asked him why he smiled. He was smiling, the Prince replied, because he had been thinking about one of his neighbors who, accompanied by his wife, was traveling when he observed an attractive young girl who pleased him greatly. He began to talk with her and, in turning to look at his wife, observed that someone was carrying on with her. This, said the Prince, is why I was smiling. The Duke understood the lesson he was being taught—two can play at the same game—and returned home with his army. The advice was indeed good. He arrived just in time to find that his northern frontiers were being attacked.

The tact required by the prince's sensitivity may be returned by ingratitude. The dependence of the prince on others is not always welcome to him and is often unrewarded. Commynes pointed out that princes prefer those who are obliged to them to those to whom they are obliged. It is more fortunate, says Commynes, for a man to be promoted to a great office which he little deserves than to be so promoted because the prince is under his obligation.[83] Franklin D. Roosevelt apparently did not find it easy to be generous or express gratitude to those who served him, especially if, like Farley, they were immensely popular.[84] When Harry Hopkins returned from a mission for President Truman, the latter thanked him

[82]Ibn Iskandar, p. 38.
[83]Commynes, p. 219.
[84]Moley, pp. 44–45 and 112.

warmly for his report and for having undertaken the trip despite ill health. Hopkins, who certainly had great loyalty to Roosevelt, remarked to a Truman aide that this was the first time he had ever been thanked for performing an arduous mission.[85]

Anger toward subordinates is not an emotion recommended for leaders; they are thought to have a special need to maintain perfect control, at least over the external expression of their emotions. President Johnson is said to have sometimes treated his staff in a patronizing fashion and to have got angry with them. Sorensen remarked that President Johnson told him, "You'll find as you get to know me better that I treat my staff just as though they were my own children."[86] This freedom to express emotion was no proper attribute of a leader to an Indian chief serving under Montcalm who, when the general became angry with him, coldly remarked: "You command, and yet you can become angry?"[87]

It is, of course, not only the ruler or leader who may be abrasive. The adviser, too, may have some of the vigor, independence, and arrogance that is thought to be more characteristic of those in the top position. Such personalities, General de Gaulle has pointed out, are likely to be passed over because they are too conscious of their own strength to let their conduct be influenced by a mere wish to please those who rule. The latter do not always realize that asperity may be one aspect of a strong character. The leader, noted de Gaulle, "can only lean on something that offers resistance."[88]

Confidence and Loyalty

A leader or ruler must have a substantial measure of confidence in his advisers if they are to be useful to him. Richelieu considered the king's confidence in his counselors as the first and absolutely necessary condition if they were to work together for the betterment of his realm.[89] This confidence, however, need not be absolute,

[85]Miller, p. 209.

[86]Sorenson, 1969, p. 96.

[87]Chamfort, p. 338. Montcalm was the general in command of the French forces that faced Wolfe at Quebec. Both he and Wolfe died in this battle.

[88]de Gaulle, p. 43.

[89]Richelieu, *Political Testament*, p. 62.

and those who wrote books of advice for the prince occasionally, but not too often, advised the prince to listen carefully and then to make up his own mind. Unless he shows a certain reserve with respect to the advice he receives, he may be viewed as simply the pawn of his ministers.

In the East, mutual confidence was not easily established. "Never be completely dependent upon [your vizier's] counsel. Hearken to what he has to say about persons or about the course to be taken in any affair, but do not make an immediate reply. Say, 'Let us consider the matter, after which we will issue appropriate commands.' Then make inquiry . . . to ascertain if it is your welfare he is seeking or his own benefit, and when all is known to you give him such reply as you think proper. Thus he will be unable to regard you as being governed by his views." The reserved attitude recommended here goes considerably further: the ruler should make certain that his vizier is unable to take a drink of water without the ruler knowing it. That this represents a generalized distrust among all members of the political class is apparent from the fact that the same book of advice recommends to the vizier that he, in turn, keep the ruler under close surveillance and inform himself "of every breath that he draws."[90]

When the adviser also serves, as he often does, as an agent and representative of the ruler, often in circumstances where the adviser is essentially on his own, the confidence required is even greater. It is a convincing confirmation of the confidence that President Wilson had in Colonel House and President Roosevelt in Hopkins that these two men were sent on missions of the highest importance, one without any instructions and the other without any written memorandum from his president. "I am going on one of the most important missions anyone ever undertook," wrote Colonel House in his diary, "and yet there is no word of direction, advice, or discussion between us. He [Wilson] knows that our minds are generally parallel, and he also knows that where they diverge I will follow his bent rather than my own. . . ."[91] Similarly, Roosevelt had absolute confidence that Hopkins in his foreign missions would not take any steps that Roosevelt had not charted.

---

[90]Ibn Iskandar, pp. 214, 223, and 235.

[91]House, vol. 4, p. 88.

"I ask you," Roosevelt wrote to Stalin, "to treat him with the identical confidence you would feel if you were talking directly to me."[92]

Since it was possible for the president of the United States to proceed in international discussions without the need to consult Washington, it was also possible for his advisers to do so when he had given them freedom of action. This contrasts with the position of a British prime minister, and consequently of his private advisers, who must report to and consult with at least the inner cabinet. To be sure, it has been observed that British prime ministers have increasingly acted as if they were operating within a presidential regime.

Advisers, ministers, and diplomats who mediate between rulers sometimes find themselves displaced by their masters who are eager to engage in direct negotiation. No writer on political life has spoken more firmly against this practice ('summitry') than Commynes whose experience with Louis XI and the Duke of Burgundy convinced him that "two great princes who wish to remain on friendly terms should never see each other but send good and wise men to one another. . . ."[93] Dean Rusk captured one of the reasons why summitry may be bad practice. "The direct confrontation of the chiefs of government of the great powers involves an extra tension because the court of last resort is in session."[94] Commynes, however, acutely observed that it was not simply the intervention of the rulers themselves that was problematic. The confrontation of their large entourages precipitated just as many or more tensions.[95] The Norwegian *King's Mirror* confirms Commynes' obser-

[92]Sherwood, p. 4.

[93]Commynes, p. 110. See also pp. 135 seq. and pp. 141–142.

[94]Dean Rusk, "The President," *Foreign Affairs*, April 1960, p. 365.

[95]"The Germans were offended by the pompous and ceremonious language of the duke which they took for pride; the Burgundians were offended by the Emperor's mean entourage and poor clothes. These disputes developed so much that they led to the war over Neuss. . . . Their servants cannot refrain from speaking about past events—one or other is sure to take offense; it is not possible for the servants and retinue of one not to be better than the other, which results in mockery. . . . When there are two different nations, their languages and clothes are different and that which pleases one does not please the other. Of two princes, one is bound to be more polite and personable to men than the other . . . and this can only reflect badly on the other." Commynes, pp. 144–145.

vations on the role of the king's retainers and aides in both bringing the king himself into disrepute at royal meetings and in exacerbating tensions between the two sides. "Everyone watches closely the behavior of all the others. And if one of the kings or one of his principal men is found indecorous, he soon becomes the subject of ridicule and contempt and is regarded as a common churl. And if a king's retinue is found to be poorly trained and is lacking in polish, especially if the service of the king's apartments is not performed in a comely and proper manner, then the king himself is pronounced unfit. . . ."[96] The danger that one of the parties might attempt to seize the other was substantial and also recommended against summitry.[97]

Talleyrand wanted Louis XVIII to take over negotiations with the allied powers in order to get the best conditions for France. Louis replied, however, that for him to become a negotiator while an army of occupation was in France was an affront to his dignity and the negotiations must be confided to ministers.[98] President Kennedy was not put off from arranging a meeting with Khrushchev by the opposition of his secretary of state to summitry. "It is far better," he had said before his election, "that we meet at the summit than at the brink,"[99] an unfortunate statement in view of the fact that a year and a half after meeting Khrushchev at the summit in Vienna, he met him again at the brink in Cuba.

A political analyst has pointed out that the jet plane seems to have increased the tendency of chiefs of government and heads of state to try to settle by themselves issues formerly dealt with by their representatives, "not always to the benefit of the questions involved."[100] Indeed it is true that the sixties saw an extraordinary amount of movement of chiefs of state and heads of government. Lack of confidence in lesser levels of contact was not, however, a principal motive in many of these confrontations at the highest levels. Political self-promotion of the leader and national public relation campaigns often count heavily in the decision to engage in summitry.

---

[96]*The King's Mirror*, p. 178.
[97]Commynes, p. 110. See also Montaigne, vol. 1, pp. 28–35.
[98]Langeron, p. 50.
[99]Schlesinger, 1965, p. 305.
[100]Alexander L. Ratcliffe, p. 617.

In earlier periods loyalty was, as we have seen (pp. 76–82), often at issue when the adviser could exploit foreign opportunities for service and desert one master for another. Loyalty was also at stake in the willingness of an adviser to speak unpleasant truths, although this form of loyalty might not be encouraged by his ruler. "Who knows but speaks not, is not loyal," said Han Fei Tzu.[101] From earliest times loyalty was also perceived as the adviser's willingness to permit the ruler to take public credit for benefits due to his advice and to accept the blame for acts committed by his master. In the *Book of History* we read, "If you have an excellent scheme or a creditable project . . . then say: 'This scheme or this project is due to my Prince's virtue.' Verily! If Ministers would all imitate this practice, how good and illustrious they would be!"[102] Bacon also warns kings that they should "make it appear to the world that the decrees and final directions . . . proceeded from themselves; and not only from their authority, but (the more to add reputation to themselves) from their head and device."[103] President Truman noted that Bernard Baruch always saw to it that his suggestions and recommendations, not always requested by the president, were given publicity, and spoke of Baruch as building a reputation on a "self-assumed" status as adviser.[104]

Much of Colonel House's ability to avoid political enmities and to maintain excellent relations with President Wilson in the early years of their relation was due to his avoidance of publicity. When a brief biography appeared that gave him full credit for his influence, the book was withdrawn at his request.[105] It is possible, of course, for modesty and the avoidance of publicity to take such extreme forms that an opposite motive may be suspected. Certainly Colonel House's efforts to conceal his importance became itself a subject of publicity.[106] House's role as *éminence grise* was paralleled

[101]Han Fei Tzu, vol. 1, p. 1.

[102]*Shu King*, p. 262.

[103]Bacon, "Of Counsel," *Selected Writings*, p. 56.

[104]Truman, vol. 2, p. 10.

[105]House, vol. 1, p. 5.

[106]In his *Philip Dru*, House pictured Senator Selwyn as a man who "wanted to govern the Nation with an absolute hand, and yet not be known as the directing power." *Philip Dru*, p. 87. Mrs. Wilson charged in her memoirs that House engaged in clandestine self-publicization at Paris. Edith Bolling Wilson, pp. 250–251.

in England by that of Maurice Hankey who was so self-effacing that when House first went to England after war broke out and made contact with all the British leaders he thought important, he was ignorant of Hankey's role in the government.[107]

An element of disloyalty may creep into the adviser-advisee relationship when the adviser seeks to manipulate his principal, perhaps 'for his own good.' Several Mirrors of Kings recommended that the adviser study the personality of his ruler in order better to get his advice accepted and in order to consolidate his relations with him. Ibn Khaldun has a similar recommendation.[108] Much of this seems proper and guileless since it is evident that it is desirable to understand the man for whom one works. Bacon, however, saw the matter differently and protested that the personality of the adviser's prince was no business of the adviser. "The true composition of a counsellor, is rather to be skilled in his master's business than his nature; for then he is likely to advise him, and not to feed his humor."[109]

It was not uncommon in the Renaissance to view state policy as an expression of the arbitary will of the ruler rather than as issuing from enduring interests of the state. This put a premium on knowledge or guesses concerning the personal inclinations of rulers and how these might be manipulated or at least taken account of. Perhaps just because manipulation of a foreign prince based on a knowledge of his person was a defensive or hostile act, manipulation of one's own ruler based on knowledge of him may have seemed a debatable activity. But even when intentions are of the best, study of the leader's character in order to deal more effectively with him borders on an affront to his dignity. When 'Abd-al-Hamîd recommended in a kindly way investigation of the character of the prince by his advisers, he revealed this affront by adding, "You know that a person who is in charge of an animal and understands his job, endeavors to know the character of the animal."[110]

A more serious source of difficulty between the political leader and his adviser ensues from any attempt that the adviser may make

---

[107]Devlin, p. 281.

[108]Ibn Khaldun, *The Muqaddimah*, vol. 2, p. 32.

[109]Bacon, "Ornamenta Rationalia," *Essays* (1883 ed.), p. 421.

[110]Ibn Khaldun, *The Muqaddimah*, vol. 2, p. 32.

to arrogate to himself authority or decisions not delegated to him by the ruler. Certainly some rulers are quite content to have others take initiatives for them. President Eisenhower is a relevant case. President Truman, on the contrary, was extremely sensitive to any attempt to infringe on presidential terrain. His *Memoirs* comment sharply on some secretaries of state who had the illusion that they were the president.[111] President Truman's relations with Secretary Acheson were excellent, but he found it necessary on one occasion to take Secretary Byrnes severely to task for issuing a policy statement without consultation with him.[112]

Some advisers and ministers become so powerful and so indispensable that the rulers they serve relinquish all authority to them. Bismarck and Metternich are cases in point. Bismarck used to insist that even in the later years of William I's life, he was only executing a policy accepted by his emperor, but when William II attempted to act as if this were really the case, a clash occurred and Bismarck was forced out.[113]

Some political leaders are fortunate enough to inspire a degree of loyalty and self-sacrifice that precludes rivalry between them and their advisers. Louis McHenry Howe sacrificed "personal fortune, fame, family, even health" in the single-minded pursuit of making Franklin D. Roosevelt president of the United States.[114] At a time when Harry Hopkins had an enormous personal investment in the Civil Works Administration, he was required by Roosevelt to liquidate the organization that provided jobs and to return to direct relief. This he did without complaint and implemented Roosevelt's directive without a murmur despite the shock of this directive to himself and his associates.[115]

It is generally assumed that the adviser owes his political leader either obedience or, if he cannot give it, his resignation, but this principle has often been honored in the breach. At times outright disobedience has been viewed as a virtue of men willing to accept full responsibility for disobeying an explicit order. Charles de Gaulle emphasized that those who have done great deeds have often had

---

[111]Truman, vol. 1, p. 547.
[112]Ibid., vol. 1, p. 550.
[113]Eyck, p. 180.
[114]Moley, pp. 132–142.
[115]Sherwood, p. 56.

to take the risk of ignoring routine aspects of discipline. Several of his examples suggest conflicts that go beyond "routine discipline." After the battle of Jutland, Jellicoe failed to seize the opportunity to destroy the German fleet. "Admiral Fisher, then First Sea Lord, exclaimed in a fury after reading Jellicoe's dispatch: 'He has all Nelson's qualities but one: he doesn't know how to disobey!'"[116] Only success can adequately justify disobedience, although some rulers have punished advisers and ministers who disobeyed them even though the results were highly favorable. Metternich was generous in this respect and not only tolerated but praised his ambassadors who deviated from instructions, an understandable tolerance in a period when rapid communication was not available to make known important changes of circumstances.[117]

Disloyalty almost necessarily implies a greater loyalty to some alternative principle or person. In earlier centuries, religious beliefs and loyalties often took priority over loyalty to the ruler. Sir Thomas More paid with his life for this form of disloyalty. The more the adviser feels himself to be the keeper of the king's conscience, as in ancient China, the more he will feel that his real loyalty is and ought to be to his moral ideals or to the people. Retirement, if not anticipated by execution, was a normal response to such conflicts. In the contemporary world, adherence to certain political, economic, or humanitarian ideals may, on the contrary, lead to conflicts in which the adviser, instead of resigning, essentially engages in a power conflict with his political leader. Lord Rothschild, confidential adviser to Prime Minister Edward Heath, and chief of the Central Policy Review Staff, did not feel called on to resign before he sharply criticized in public important projects strongly supported by his prime minister. Opinions may differ on the propriety of such behavior by a top civil servant, but within the cabinet itself it is clear that he who cannot support government policy owes his leader either silence or resignation.

Party loyalties are often thought, even where patronage considerations do not exist, to make it difficult for a member of one party

---

[116]de Gaulle, p. 45.

[117]In 1822, a letter from Vienna to Paris by special courier generally took seven days, by ordinary post ten or eleven days. To capitals like Constantinople and Moscow, weeks were required. Sauvigny, pp. 97–98.

to be completely loyal to a political leader of an opposing party. Presidents, however, have not infrequently made major appointments from among members of the opposite party. President Kennedy appointed Douglas Dillon to the Treasury although warned by his brother that in so doing they were putting themselves in the hands of a Republican who had no reason for loyalty to them and might betray them. Robert Kennedy asked Dillon what he would do if he felt himself in disagreement with administration policy, and when Dillon replied that if he had to resign, he would, of course, go quietly, the appointment was made.[118]

Scientists and other intellectuals may feel that they owe loyalty above all to certain principles cherished within the intellectual or scientific community. In fact, breaches between scientists and political leaders have often involved conflicts over moral and political principles rather than over those thought to be particular to the scientific community. The ABM controversy in the United States (see p. 101) illustrates this process. In any case, scientists, too, have the expedient of resigning when a conflict of conscience occurs.

Another alternative loyalty which may conflict with loyalty to the ruler is the adviser's pursuit of his own material gain, security, prestige, or power. "The first condition of a good Counsellour," said Hobbes, is "that his Ends, and Interest, be not inconsistent with the Ends and Interest of him he Counselleth."[119] This is often a difficult condition to fulfill. Confucius noted that those who serve the ruler "before obtaining their position . . . are in anxiety to obtain it, and when they have it they are in anxiety lest they lose it; and if men are in anxiety about losing their position, there is no length to which they will not go."[120]

The Risk of Being an Adviser

The subservience and flattery shown princes often seemed designed to ward off the fear and horror aroused by too close an association with a great and arbitrary power. That such apprehen-

[118]Schlesinger, 1965, p. 136. On the role of resignation as a form of protest in the U.S. political system, see E. Weisband and T. M. Franck.

[119]Hobbes, p. 137.

[120]Confucius, *Analects*, bk. 17, chap. 15.

sions were entirely justified is amply illustrated by the simple fact that eleven of the advisers discussed in this volume suffered death, prison, or torture.[121] Han Fei Tzu conveys something of the emotions aroused by proximity to absolute power when he speaks of the sovereign as a dragon; men can sometimes tame it, play with it, and ride on its back. But below its throat are very sensitive scales, and anyone who touches them dies.[122] To attend on the emperor, says a Chinese proverb, is like sleeping with a tiger.[123] For Kautilya, life in the service of a king is equivalent to living in fire.[124] Juvenal describes the members of the Emperor Domitian's Privy Council "each of whom quailed beneath the Emperor's hatred, whose drawn white faces reflected that great and perilous 'friendship.'" Ibn Iskandar asks, "How can a man who has acquaintance with kings lay himself down to sleep free of care?"[125] Han Fei Tzu, speaking of the difficulty faced by advisers who seek to guide the ruler, recites a catalogue of horrors taken from the lives of ministers in the service of the Chinese states. These ministers were broiled, had their hearts cut open, were pickled in brine, had their feet cut off, were dismembered, and stoned to death. Lord Shang was pulled apart by horses. This predilection for torture rather than simple execution is not universal, but similar examples can be drawn from the history of political advisers in a variety of societies. The relatively humane and dignified deaths of Seneca and Sir Thomas More were the least that some political experts had to fear.

Machiavelli devotes a chapter of his *Discourses* to "The Danger of Being Prominent in Counselling." In counseling an enterprise of great importance, the blame of failure is charged to him who first advised it, and success rarely reaps a reward that equals the potential punishment.[126] Motse affirms that among those who excel there are few who do not perish on account of it.[127]

Advisers who predict disagreeable things to their masters can

---

[121]Aesop, Boethius, Shang Yang, Han Fei Tzu, Seneca, Commynes, Don Juan Manuel, Ibn Khaldun, Machiavelli, Sir Thomas More, Bacon.

[122]Han Fei Tzu, vol. 1., p. 112.

[123]Scarborough, p. 191.

[124]Shamasastry, *Kautilya's Arthasastra*, p. 283.

[125]Ibn Iskandar, p. 45.

[126]Machiavelli, *The Discourses*, pp. 513–515.

[127]Motse, p. 4.

be taught to improve their vision by the threat of prison and death.[128] India showed a gentler attitude toward erroneous predictions: "Whoever has made three errors in his practice of divination receives no other punishment except that for the future he is compelled to be silent; and there is no one who can compel that man to speak, upon whom the judgment of silence has been passed."[129]

Hobbes protested that whosoever gives counsel should not be punished for it, for whoever asks for counsel is the real author of it. However, when an adviser provides "counsell vehemently pressed" this display of emotion suggests that the service is being offered more for the benefit of the adviser than of the recipient.[130]

In the contemporary world, those who stand close to the dragon's scales continue to have reason to fear the consequences of this proximity, dangerous both because of the ruler's displeasure and because the adviser may share the fate that often overtakes those at the pinnacle of power, as did President Nixon's advisers. Advisers who are farther from top political positions but who provide technical or political advice in the varied areas of government action also run risks that to them may seem equally grave—responsibility for incorrect decisions, loss of appointment, and damage to their professional reputations. Committee and corporate forms of advice giving sometimes mitigate the risks of individuals, but this result can only be achieved if the individual does not make too vigorous or idiosyncratic a contribution. The committee procedure "stresses avoidance of risk rather than boldness of conception."[131] Probably this is so because in case of failure the individual is still likely to be blamed, but in case of success it will often be the committee or corporate group that will be praised or benefit.

---

[128] *Comprehensive Discussions in the White Tiger Hall*, vol. 1, p. 121.
[129] Arrian, *The Indica*, p. 740.
[130] Hobbes, p. 135.
[131] Kissinger, 1960, p. 344.

5

Decision Making and the Adviser

Action and Inaction

Few problems can be so troublesome to the adviser and his principal as choosing when to act and when not to act. The difficulty of this question is reflected in the opposing views expressed on this matter in the manuals of statecraft and in other discussions of the political art.

Three major answers are provided to the question, sometimes several by the same writer, another indication of the difficulties of the problem.

In one view, there is an exact moment to act—one moment earlier is a moment too soon, one moment later is a moment too late. This outlook, productive of great anxiety in the decision maker afflicted with it, and related to the proverb "opportunity knocks only once," can be modified in two ways—one, by increasing the "moment" from a more to a less demanding interval of time; two, by affirming that while there is a most favorable moment for action, slightly less favorable time points do not necessarily doom one to failure; they may simply impose higher costs to achieve the desired goal.

Typically the right moment is lost by too great a delay. The Chinese legists, proponents of bold and decisive action, were not prone to this error. Li Ssu, onetime colleague and enemy of Han Fei Tzu, in his memorial to the ruler of Ch'in, destined to unify China, warned: "He who waits on others misses his opportunities, while a man aiming at great achievements takes advantage of a critical juncture and relentessly follows it through. . . . This is the one moment in ten thousand ages. If Your Highness allows it to slip away and does not press the advantage in haste, the feudal lords will revive their strength and organize themselves into an anti-Ch'in alliance."[1] In Lie tseu we read that failure may come from not finding "the favorable moment." Success follows the choice of "the opportune moment."[2] For Kautilya, too, opportunity offers itself only once and he who waits for it to come a second time will wait in vain.[3] Guez de Balzac, in his book *Le Prince*, in praise of Louis XIII, warns, "One must recognize the appropriate moment. . . . All human actions have their right moment, for even the most virtuous may be done inopportunely."[4] Like Cavour, whom he admired, Colonel House was said to wait "for the supreme moment" and then to risk everything.[5] In French politics the success of the political leader is thought to depend in good part on his ability to discern *le moment-top*, that is the precise moment before which action would be too soon and after which it would be too late.[6] Eleanor Roosevelt wrote that President Roosevelt "could watch with enormous patience as a situation developed and would wait for exactly the right moment to act." Waiting for the right moment may be or may seem to be an excuse for postponing a decision. Roosevelt on occasion impressed observers as having a penchant for postponement.[7]

A second position, not too far removed from the first attitude, condemns delay and irresolution and shows a generalized preference for action. There is, perhaps, no invariable association be-

---

[1]*Sources of Chinese Tradition*, pp. 153–154.
[2]Lie tseu, *Le Vrai Classique . . .*, p. 188.
[3]Shamasastry, *Kautilya's Arthasastra*, p. 287.
[4]Church, p. 37.
[5]House, vol. 1, p. 11.
[6]Melnik and Leites, p. 23.
[7]Schlesinger, 1959, p. 529.

tween speed of decision and preference for action, but the two attitudes are often found together. We shall see below, conversely, that the propensity to delay is associated with a distrust of, or distaste for, action. This relation derives in part from the fact that few men are gifted equally in counsel and in action. Thucydides tells us that Pericles was "the first man of his time at Athens, ablest alike in counsel and in action."[8] But more commonly those who are talented in foreseeing dangers when engaged in counsel and deliberation are not able to suppress this talent to the degree required when action must be undertaken. "Boldness is . . . ill in counsel, but good in execution."[9] In counsel the bold man likes to call for action but often is vague in suggesting specific policies or plans, a fault for which Nestor gently chided "the bold Diomedes."[10]

Intolerance of delay and preference for action are associated with an impatience with "talk." Motse did not want to listen to those who talked much but were slow in action, or who kept talking about things that could not be implemented, which was "merely to wear out one's mouth."[11] Similarly the emperor's Lord Grand Secretary told the scholars, in a debate on ancient Chinese commercial and industrial policy, that "talk is easy, but to act is difficult" and "the Literati are capable of speech, but incapable in action."[12] For Metternich, in diplomacy, "Nothing more easily causes harm than long discussions." What is important is clear, exact language and not the quantity of it.[13] Although as talkative as many other political types, if not more so, Bolsheviks claimed to be—perhaps for that reason—distrustful of talk and stressed the importance of action. Lenin appealed "for *decisions* and not talk; for *actions*, not writing resolutions. . . ." And again, "Enough of idle talk! . . . We need action and action!"[14] Similar complaints are sometimes made about academics. Thus a government official testified before a Sen-

---

[8]Thucydides, p. 79.

[9]Bacon, "Ornamenta Rationalia," *Essays* (1883 ed.), p. 420.

[10]*The Iliad*, bk. IX.

[11]Motse, pp. 7 and 217.

[12]*Discourses on Salt and Iron*, pp. 45 and 103.

[13]Sauvigny, p. 88.

[14]Cited in Leites, 1953, p. 218. See also chap. VI, pt. 3, "The Danger of Merely Talking," pp. 215–225.

ate subcommittee that the social scientist is "inclined to plead for further research before committing himself" and that "some liberal and distinguished social scientists" feel that their principal goal should be to "emphasize the profundity of our socio-economic problems so that the public will understand why these problems can't be solved quickly."[15] The emphasis on action and distaste for "talk" was particularly strong in Harry Hopkins, as it probably is in most persons whose advancement has been based largely on experience and administration rather than on training and sophistication in analysis. "I belong to the school that does not talk about things—you *do* them."[16] President Truman's *Memoirs* and comments on his administrative habits by others suggest a person impatient of delay. Dean Acheson remarked that making something complex out of something simple enables one to delay making up one's mind. "That was something that never troubled Mr. Truman." Truman instructed Secretary of State Acheson, if an *important* decision needed to be made, to bring it to him in the morning so he would have time to think it over—that is, to reach a decision that day.[17]

Ibn Khaldun also felt that talking "defeats accomplishment," but his concern, unlike those cited just above, was not the delay in action that talking may induce, but rather that talking may become a substitute for thinking.[18] He, presumably, would not have favored committee deliberations.

A primary motive for avoiding delay in initiating action derives from the dual fact that action is often a response to disagreeable developments, and these developments often become more difficult to handle with the passage of time. Machiavelli condemned the hesitations of those who let disorders grow: "war is not thereby avoided, but only deferred to your disadvantage."[19] The Romans never cared for what "is now every day to be heard in the mouths of our wise men, namely to enjoy the advantages of delay . . . for time . . . may produce indifferently either good or evil."[20] "Take

---

[15]Gorham, p. 73.
[16]Sherwood, p. 160.
[17]Miller, pp. 242 and 385.
[18]Ibn Khaldun, *The Muqaddimah*, vol. 2, p. 34.
[19]Machiavelli, *The Prince*, p. 14.
[20]Ibid., p. 11.

energetic measures," said Botero, "at the first sign of trouble, because disorder grows and gathers strength with time."[21] In modern times, the Bolsheviks emphasized the principle that problems, especially oppositional tendencies, must be dealt with immediately, that is, must be "nipped in the bud."[22]

Delay and the avoidance of action may be seen as a failure of political responsibility and loss of nerve. "All knowledge consisteth in action," said Grimaldus. Without action, the "wisdome of a solitary citizen is no more profitable than the treasure of a covetous man buried in the ground."[23] Part of the attraction of Machiavelli to political minds such as Spinoza, Sidney, and Harrington was his defense of political activism and his conviction that it is possible to gain control over one's political fate.[24] Bacon felt that he was more fit to read and write books than he was to play a part in politics, but that nonetheless he had given his life to civil causes because "in this theatre of man's life it is reserved only for God and Angels to be lookers-on."[25]

A third outlook shows a preference for inaction and consequently a tolerance for delay and temporizing. Intervention in the ongoing events of the world may be viewed as either dangerous or futile. In Eastern cultures both the importance of cultivating one's own inner resources, convictions concerning an inexorable fate and the omnipotence of inaction were hardly favorable to intervention and energetic action. "Now all is confused, all is obscure. . . . It is thus both for those who act and for those who do not act. . . . Who knows why? All this is inexorable. . . . Why go? Why come? Why be sad? Why be gay? Why act? Why not act?"[26]

A reserved attitude toward intervention and action may be based on a less radical denial of man's capacity to direct affairs, and on a belief that much that man wishes to achieve is much better effected by time. Emerson deplored "the waste of strength in gathering unripe fruits. . . . A little time will do more than the most puissant

---

[21]Botero, p. 41.
[22]See Leites, 1953, pp. 55–56 and 449–461.
[23]Grimaldus, pp. 47 and 59.
[24]Fleisher, p. 116.
[25]Bacon, *Selected Writings*, p. xxviii.
[26]Lie tseu, *Le Vrai Classique . . .* , p. 174.

genius."[27] Such views played an important role in debates on the political craft. Although Machiavelli condemned delay in dealing with disorders, he believed that there are times when it is desirable to temporize. It is sometimes difficult to know the precise character of evils when they first arise. In these cases "the wiser course is to temporize . . . instead of violently attacking them; for by temporizing with them they will either die out of themselves, or at least their worst result will be long deferred. And princes or magistrates . . . must not believe that a fire can be extinguished by blowing upon it." After this cautionary note, Machiavelli reverts to his earlier position and adds, "If they think themselves sufficiently strong to combat it, then they should attack it regardless of consequences; otherwise they should let it be, and in no wise attempt it."[28] Botero takes a similar line. Having also recommended energetic measures at the first sign of trouble, he adds, "But when the trouble is too great for your strength, play for time, because with time circumstances change and where there is time there is still life."[29] Guicciardini had only a qualified respect for Renaissance proverbs and maxims concerning the benefits of time and delay. In Florence, a policy of delay, of hoping for more favorable circumstances, combined with political skill, was a conscious form of statecraft deliberately chosen in light of the military weakness of the city.[30] For Guicciardini, opportunity knocks just once and in many cases it is necessary to decide and to act quickly. "But when you are in difficult straits or involved in troublesome affairs, procrastinate, and wait as long as you can. For often time will enlighten or free you. Using the proverb thus, it is always salutary. But understood differently, it could be harmful."[31]

The attitude that the passage of time may do more than human intervention is by no means absent from modern political maxims. Metternich stressed that "calmness is more advantageous in avoid-

[27]Emerson, p. 98.

[28]Machiavelli, *The Discourses*, p. 200.

[29]Botero, p. 41. Botero says that long deliberations are best for rulers of great territories since their concern is to preserve rather than to conquer. But quick decisions, that is boldness, are best for those intent on increasing their dominions. Ibid., p. 50.

[30]Felix Gilbert, p. 34.

[31]Guicciardini, *Maxims*, p. 61.

ing complications than an excess of activity." Again, "the endeavours of men generally only hinder the natural course of events: so that when what is natural corresponds to what is desirable, there must be no movement." And again, "my practice is to wait for natural forces to arrange matters." Metternich, however, also stressed an important qualification: time benefits only those whose position is correct and strong. While these seem to be his predominant views, they did not preclude Metternich from writing to the Duke of Wellington: "Whenever men who are responsible for important matters of State allow themselves to wait for fate to lead them, things go wrong. . . ."[32]

A writer of a modern manual of diplomacy also draws attention to the virtues of nonintervention. "Time . . . will often solve problems without having a diplomat rush in with both arms waving"; good precepts to keep in mind are "When in doubt do nothing" and "Doing nothing is better than doing the wrong thing."[33] In the sixties, Italians took themselves as a prime confirmation of the value of the maxim: "No policy is the best policy."[34] Henry Kissinger, however, draws attention to dangers in the belief that a machine called "history" evolves, regardless of the diplomat's will, a self-implementing policy. The awareness in 1813 that Napoleon's empire was tottering was not in itself a policy but the condition of a policy that had to be formulated and implemented.[35]

Irresolution and delay is sometimes thought to be a deficiency of political leaders and advisers of an analytic and academic turn of mind. "The President's [Wilson] penchant for inaction makes him hesitate to take the plunge."[36] But even of so great a king as Henry II, Giraldus could complain ". . . his decisions on all proceedings were dilatory."[37] And so great a statesman as Richelieu was said to be irresolute in action and to have required the assistance of Father Joseph, his aide and adviser, in avoiding compromise and delay.[38] Adlai Stevenson damaged his political careeer by im-

---

[32]Sauvigny, pp. 83–84 and 110.
[33]Bailey, pp. 141–142.
[34]Goldhamer, p. 70.
[35]Kissinger, 1957, p. 324.
[36]House, vol. 2, p. 229.
[37]Giraldus, *Conquest of Ireland*, bk. I, chap. 45.
[38]Callières, p. 30.

pressing a variety of political figures, including Presidents Truman and Kennedy, as irresolute.[39]

Delay does not necessarily signify indecision. It may represent the prudence required when great stakes are at issue. When the English at Agincourt were crying "Forward, forward," eager to open the battle, and the Dukes of Clarence, Gloucester, and York were urging the same upon Henry V, "yet the King stayed a while, lest any jeopardy were not foreseen, or any hazard not prevented."[40] This was not a trivial virtue, for a certain inconsequence, noble high spiritedness, and idea of honor often tended to hasten action beyond the limits of prudence. In the Middle Ages many battles were lost by rash attacks provoked by taunts of cowardice made by reckless knights.[41] The Mirrors of Kings were not providing supererogatory advice when they insisted that "it is very important for a prince to think before acting."[42] "I did not think," said Erasmus, is not a fit expression for a wise man, and still less for a prince. A young prince rashly begins a war that lasts twenty years, at length recovers his senses and says "I did not think." "That sort of wisdom is too expensive for the state."[43]

The advisers of rulers have sometimes shown an exemplary insistence that their princes avoid wars and battles. Commynes was much pleased that his prudent master did not place "his own position as King of this great and obedient realm of France in peril by a thing so uncertain as a battle."[44] Commynes was with Louis on one of the few occasions when news arrived of a lost battle. The king was very grieved because normally "he never risked anything and never hankered after battles—nor was this one waged at his command."[45] According to Giraldus, Henry II "so much feared the doubtful fortune [of war] that . . . he tried all courses before he resorted to arms."[46]

Guez de Balzac pointed out that the King of France and the

---

[39]Truman, vol. 2, p. 496 and Schlesinger, 1965, p. 9.
[40]Holinshed, pp. 553b–554a.
[41]Norman, p. 144.
[42]Born, 1928a, p. 488.
[43]Erasmus, pp. 155–156.
[44]Commynes, p. 96.
[45]Ibid., p. 380.
[46]Giraldus, *Conquest of Ireland*, bk. I, chap. 45.

King of Spain were too powerful to ruin each other; wars resulted from the bad counsel they received from ministers who wanted to keep the nobles away from the court in order to enhance their own power and cause many deaths so that they would have offices to fill. "It is folly for a prince to make war except in great necessity. . . . The maxim that we teach—that even an unjust peace is better than war—is not a trivial or vulgar saying. . . ."[47]

Lord Shang, who could scarcely be said to lack boldness, was not inclined to ignore the virtues of prudence in matters where much was at stake. "The great rule of an army is prudence." The enemy should only be attacked if he is "in every way your inferior."[48] Machiavelli provided identical advice: "But what must be observed with the very greatest care is never to lead an army into combat when it has the very least doubt of victory."[49] And even more emphatically: "A good leader never risks a battle if he is not forced into it by necessity or if the occasion does not require it."[50] This prudence is equally applicable to political battles. Metternich "never fought a battle he was not certain of winning. . . ."[51]

Prudence can, of course, degenerate into the avoidance of necessary action, especially if the leader adheres rigorously to the maxim to engage himself only when sure of victory. Prudence of this sort has become synonymous with caution. In Machiavelli's time the traditional meaning of *prudenza* was the application of calm calculation and practical reason to issues requiring decisions. Prudence was simply adopting the right course to realize one's purpose.[52]

Prudence in the sense of caution may be developed to the point where the capacity to make decisions is greatly hampered. When this is combined with fear of responsibility, the individual is no longer in any useful sense a decision maker. General Marshall said that the ability to make a decision is perhaps the greatest gift a man can have. And Secretary Acheson, referring to this remark, rated President Truman's willingness and ability to decide as his

---

[47]Church, p. 51.
[48]Shang, p. 245.
[49]Machiavelli, *L'Art de la guerre*, p. 825.
[50]Ibid., p. 894.
[51]Kissinger, 1957, p. 323.
[52]Fleisher, pp. 139–140.

greatest quality as president and as a leader.[53] President Franklin D. Roosevelt was proud of a calculation that showed he had made some thirty-five or more decisions for every one made by President Coolidge.[54]

Perhaps it is the fateful character of the decisions that they must take that leads military men to be especially sensitive to the irrevocable character of human intervention in events. General de Gaulle noted that when Pétain was asked what part of action called for the greatest effort, he replied, "Giving orders." A decision, added de Gaulle, requires a moral as well as an intellectual effort.[55]

The Analytic Mind

Analysis, calculation, rationality, efficiency, planning, theory, and related terms represent dispositions in the treatment of decision problems that are sometimes viewed as a peculiarly modern, one might almost say contemporary, development. Certainly no age can rival our own in the creation of sophisticated intellectual devices, mechanical aids, and imposing institutions and organizations for the study and resolution of policy questions. Nonetheless, earlier ages have also shown their own awareness and appreciation of the role of calculation and analysis in the decision process. The conflict between the rival claims of what Pascal in the mid-seventeenth century called *l'esprit de géométrie* and *l'esprit de finesse*, that is between the mathematical or analytic mind and the intuitive mind, between the claims of calculation and those of wisdom and experience, is as old as discussions of the political process and still continues today.

Pascal characterized the mathematical mind as one that prefers a limited number of definitions, axioms, premises, or principles from which it is possible to derive further propositions by a clear and inexorable logic.[56] I shall take a broader view and characterize the mathematical, rationalizing, or analytic mind by several preferences beyond that noted by Pascal.

---

[53]Miller, p. 378.
[54]Schlesinger, 1959, p. 527.
[55]de Gaulle, pp. 26–27.
[56]Pascal, pp. 1–3.

The rationalizing, analytic disposition in politics showed itself, in some instances, as a rejection of or skepticism regarding the role of the supernatural in political life. Divination, oracles, avenging deities, and other manifestations of the supernatural were rejected in favor of man's own rational resources. The rationalizing mind also saw traditional wisdom and its accompanying preferences for old institutional forms and rituals, as in ancient China, as obstructing the recognition of new situations, new methods, and new solutions.

A more positive manifestation of the analytic mind was its passion for efficiency, its corresponding distaste for 'waste' and the introduction of criteria to promote the former and avoid the latter. Motse, who had a strong rationalizing disposition, attacked the expensive funerals and the long periods of mourning, dictated by ritual and tradition, that imposed serious economic costs on the individual and society.[57] This sensitivity to 'waste,' characteristic of persons with an implicit if not explicit cost-benefit outlook, is equally reflected in Colonel House's anonymous Utopian novel, *Philip Dru: Administrator*. In this short book devoted to Philip Dru's remaking of American political and economic life, Colonel House thought it worthwhile to devote a full chapter to describe his hero's abolition of wasteful, uneconomical funeral practices. In a much broader sense efficiency may mean organizing things so well that they run almost of their own accord. As Han Fei Tzu said, "If the ruler has to exert any special skill of his own, it means that affairs are not going right."[58] For him and Lord Shang the law was a mechanism that provided for impersonal, automatic operation of society.

Han Fei Tzu's conception of what today we call cost-benefit analysis led him to note that some advisers acted as if policies were possible that provided only benefits. His sense of rationality revolted against facile recommendations that excluded costs from the cost-benefit equation.[59] Erasmus appealed to cost-benefit analysis, rather than to moral arguments, when he tried to persuade the prince to "take a rational estimate long enough to reckon what the

---

[57]Waley, pp. 165–167. See also pp. 129–134.
[58]Han Fei Tzu, vol. 1, p. 53.
[59]Ibid., vol. 2, p. 239.

war will cost and whether the final end to be gained is worth that much—even if victory is certain. . . . Weigh the worries, the expenditures, the trials, the long wearisome preparation." A town, Erasmus continued, is often captured at greater labor and expense than it would cost to build a new one.[60] Metternich insisted that no matter how necessary and urgent a measure might appear and how great the benefits to be sought were, it was nonetheless necessary to ensure that they were not being attained at a still higher cost.[61]

It did not require a high order of decision theory to reach the commonplace conclusion that costs may outweigh benefits. What was more significant in this strain of thought was its accompanying emphasis on careful calculation. Such calculations called for assumptions concerning the future course of events, particularly those not readily subject to control. Those of an optimistic turn of mind felt that if action was taken only when all elements of the situation were known, success was almost certain. Failure in such circumstances represented inadequate calculations. Sun Tzu quotes the saying, "If you know the enemy and know yourself, you need not fear the result of a hundred battles. If you know yourself but not the enemy, for every victory gained, you will also suffer a defeat. If you know neither the enemy nor yourself, you will run risks in every battle." Again, "Many calculations lead to victory and few calculations to defeat. . . ."[62] This emphasis on calculation is not surprising in a society in which the first minister was in ancient days sometimes called "The Universal Calculator."[63] Those of a pessimistic or cautious turn of mind relied more largely on what today in military studies is called "worst case analysis." "I usually base my calculations," wrote Metternich, "on the possibility that everything will go wrong. . . ."[64]

The analytic mind is often intolerant of vague or colorful language. The analytic mind may not be mathematical or quantitative, but it will at least require rigor. Hobbes, although appreciative of

---

[60]Erasmus, pp. 249–250 and 254.
[61]Sauvigny, p. 111.
[62]Sun Tzu, pp. 24 and 7.
[63]*Shu King*, p. 11.
[64]Sauvigny, p. 81.

the use of "Fancy" in stirring the understanding, thought that "to admit [Metaphors] into Councell or Reasoning, were manifest folly."[65] Metternich always started "from one simple rule of calculation. . . . Anything that is good in itself must be capable of being expressed clearly and precisely. The moment I come across words that are not very clear or that are positively wrong, I am left with the conclusion that they are either *mistaken* or *deceitful*."[66]

To the analytic mind deliberation may involve an active rehearsal of future possibilities. This produces a desire for 'scenarios' and 'gaming.' Motse, a great expert on siege warfare as well as politics, is said to have persuaded an opposing general to lift the siege of a city he was defending by playing through in a 'seminar game' with his opponent their respective strategies and thereby proving that the siege would be a failure and that his opponent's knowledge of his strategy and possession of his person were taken care of by his meta-strategy. Kautilya recommended that an envoy setting off on a mission to the enemy should first rehearse what he will tell the enemy, what he thinks the enemy may then say to him, what he will then reply, and so forth.[67] This may not seem like the highest development of the rationalizing mind, but planning political behavior in its details rather than leaving it to the inspiration of the moment is not a trivial development. The same preference for forward-looking deliberation was expressed by Colonel House within a month of the onset of World War I in August 1914: "I do not believe in leaving things to chance, and then attribute failure to lack of luck or opportunity. I am trying to think out in advance the problems that the war will entail. . . ."[68]

The rationalizing mind resents the attribution of luck to what was the outcome of sustained and difficult calculation and planning. "To conquer for four generations," said Hsüntse, referring to the victories of Ch'in, "is not luck, but calculation."[69] Similarly, Polybius resented the fact that historians, in speaking of Publius Scipio, "attribute the success obtained not to the man and his foresight, but to the gods and to Fortune . . . in spite of the fact that Publius

[65]Hobbes, p. 34.

[66]Sauvigny, p. 110.

[67]Shamasastry, *Kautilya's Arthasastra*, p. 29.

[68]House, vol. 1, p. 322.

[69]Cited in Shang, p. 4.

himself in a letter addressed to Philip has distinctly set forth that it was upon the deliberate calculations, which I have just set forth, that he undertook the Iberian campaign generally, and the assault upon New Carthage in particular."[70] This recognition of calculation and planning did not signify any failure on Polybius' part to appreciate the role of the unpredictable.

A preoccupation with the unpredictable was characteristic of Florentine political thinking but was accompanied by an equal confidence that *ragione*, reason, particularly the Florentine variety, was a powerful instrument for sheltering man from the arbitrary and uncontrollable forces of *Fortuna* by which he was surrounded. Decisions resulting from the exercise of *ragione* were likely to be quite different from those resulting from 'desire' or 'will.' Guicciardini's *Discorso di Logrogno* has been called one of the earliest, if not the first, comprehensive literary work in which politics is systematically based on the criterion of rational efficiency. The existence of laws or institutions is no proof of their value; the only acceptable criterion is whether they provide the political and social effects desired.[71]

Florentine delight and confidence in the exercise of *ragione* was characteristic of an urban bourgeoisie alienated from feudal thought and confident that all things were possible to the possessor of a rational technique.[72] This exercise of political gifts reaches a special stage when it is experienced as an addiction or a personal passion. Machiavelli, writing to a colleague, confesses that he must write about "the one thing I know, politics—or else keep quiet."[73] "For a certainty, nothing is so delightful as politics," remarked Courtilz, referring to his pleasure in problems of political calculation and his readiness to calculate for any sovereign who asked him a special formula suited to that ruler's interests.[74]

The rationalizing mind is not content with devising ad hoc responses to situations as they emerge. Certain rules of behavior are

---

[70]Polybius, vol. 2, p. 8.

[71]Felix Gilbert, pp. 38, 96, and 99.

[72]von Martin, p. 20.

[73]Machiavelli, "Choix de lettres," in *Le Prince*, p. 177.

[74]Meinecke, p. 246. Courtilz (1644–1712) was the founder of the *Mercure historique et politique*, the first real political review, read by an international public interested in the secrets of the European courts. Ibid., p. 245.

necessary that will lead to specifiable results. Cicero urged the study of political cycles whose beginning it was essential to recognize "in order that we may know the tendency of each change and thus be able to retard the movement or forestall it."[75] Motse pointed out that a skilled carpenter has instruments and rules for making straight lines, circles, or a plumb line. Unskilled craftsmen may not be quite so accurate but the availability of standard procedures ensures that they get tolerable results. Generals and counselors-of-state must equally have standard procedures that will provide predictable results.[76] Lord Shang had made a beginning in providing statesmen with theorems such as "To rise to supremacy, there is a definite way, but to hold it there are different principles";[77] "In an orderly country, punishments are numerous and rewards are rare";[78] the aim of punishment is to abolish punishment;[79] if a bureaucracy is not divided into parts with diversified and conflicting interests it cannot be controlled.[80]

Rules of thumb did not satisfy later political advisers and writers. Rational political action required a knowledge of generalizations based on observations of political reality. "Nothing is worthier of human reason; nothing is more instructive or more calculated to increase the sum of our knowledge," wrote the young Frederick II, speaking of such efforts.[81] For Ibn Khaldun, the laws that describe social behavior are not as invariable as those that govern natural phenomena but sufficiently so to be useful for understanding and for political action, especially since these laws affect masses and are not much influenced by great men.[82] Machiavelli and Guicciardini would have agreed with the spirit of Ibn Khaldun's remarks but would probably have accorded great men a larger role in political history, and indeed would have seen them as in part the embodiment of those indeterminate elements in politics represented by *Fortuna*.

---

[75]Cicero, *Commonwealth*, p. 178.
[76]Motse, pp. 13–14.
[77]Shang, p. 228.
[78]Ibid., p. 230.
[79]Ibid., p. 285.
[80]Ibid., p. 321.
[81]Meinecke, p. 288.
[82]Issawi, p. 7.

The emphasis on generalization has to be understood as a reaction against those who stressed only a detailed knowledge of the situation without any guidance from historically derived principles. Machiavelli especially was critical of the failure of the humanists to reduce political history to a systematic body of knowledge as had the teachers of law and medicine.[83] Theoretical knowledge was of particular importance for the young prince since, as Erasmus pointed out, he could not as yet rely on knowledge gained from experience. This supplement to the prince's theoretical knowledge can be furnished by the advice of older men.[84]

Motse's simple proof that the future can be known may not have seemed very convincing with respect to major political events, but it illustrates his impatience with those who deny that the future can be known and yet base almost all of their day-to-day actions precisely on the assumption that they know it.[85] Some of these forms of prediction may play a major role in political decison making. Understanding human behavior and deriving from the observation of individuals predictions concerning their behavior have been important for the decisions and success of some statesmen. Metternich was conscious of his talent in this direction. "I know the moral attitude of the Emperor Alexander as well as the line that his Cabinet will follow, voluntarily or involuntarily. I also know the minds of the two Secretaries of State, their tendencies and their moral range. Consequently nothing that comes from St. Petersburg or that arises out of the doubtful points in Russian policy is capable of surprising me."[86]

The ability to predict still has a touch of magic to it, and this was even truer in the past. When Savonarola's prediction that a great

---

[83]Gilmore, p. 28.

[84]Erasmus, p. 156.

[85]"P'eng Ch'ing Shengtse said: 'The past can be known, the future cannot.' Motse said: Suppose your parents met with misfortune a hundred li away. And there was just the margin of a single day. If they could be reached they would live, if not they would die. Here are a strong wagon and an excellent horse, and also a bad horse and a square-wheeled cart. And you are allowed to choose. Which would you take? It was replied that the excellent horse and the strong wagon would of course make for a more speedy journey. Motse said: How then is the future not knowable?" Motse, p. 253.

[86]Sauvigny, p. 85.

disaster would befall Italy was fulfilled by the French invasion of 1494, his influence in Florence was greatly increased.[87]

Successful predictions cannot be taken as evidence of the power of the analytic mind since they are just as likely to have been derived by the intuitive mind basing itself on intimate and prolonged experience. Principled predictions, that is predictions based on explicitly held propositions and derived from them, can be found in political writings from ancient China to the present, but the degree of formalization both in the statement of the principles and in the rules for deriving predictions from them was so limited that this instrument was more a personal possession than a readily transferable tool. In the contemporary world, explicit models, simulation, gaming, and other devices attempt to provide the formalizations to raise prediction to the level of a transferable technique.

The disposition of the analytic mind toward formalization and rigor led almost inevitably to mathematics and quantification. Plato thought that "no single instrument of youthful education has such mighty power, both as regards domestic economy and politics, and in the arts, as the study of arithmetic."[88] But this was intended more as a form of stimulating the mind than a tool for political reasoning. While the mathematical mind, as defined by Pascal, played an important role in giving an impetus to some rationalization of the decision-making process, mathematics and mathematical statistics did not play a significant role in the decision-making process until virtually the contemporary period.

The difficulties in applying mathematics to decision making did not hold for quantification itself. The appreciation of the role of numbers in planning and political decision making is very old, as one can observe in Lord Shang. His insistence on the thirteen figures necessary for rational civil and military administration represents an extraordinary achievement. "A strong country knows thirteen figures: the number of granaries within its borders, the number of ablebodied men and of women, the number of old and of weak people, the number of officials and of officers, the number of those making a livelihood by talking, the number of useful people, the number of horses and of oxen, the quantity of fodder and

[87]Felix Gilbert, p. 56.
[88]Plato, *Laws*, bk. V (747).

of straw. If he, who wishes to make his country strong, does not know these thirteen figures, though his geographical position may be favourable and the population numerous, his state will become weaker and weaker, until it is dismembered."[89] "Statistics is the true method of ministers and rulers and the essential of a state." "The early kings," wrote Lord Shang, "did not rely on their beliefs but on their figures."[90] Han Fei Tzu is in perfect agreement. "Those who are most intelligent in governing by law, rely on statistical methods and do not rely on men [of reputation]. . . . It is because reliance is placed on statistics that, within the territory, order reigns. . . ."[91] Lord Shang was not simply promoting administrative statistics, he was arguing for the importance of measurement in all significant matters. Whoever wants to learn the depth of an abyss can do so by dropping a string and measuring its length.[92] This reaction against reliance on personal estimation and guesswork is evident in almost all phases of Lord Shang's political treatise.

Polybius expressed his appreciation for numerical calculation in the contempt he showed for a general who undertook a siege operation without having the foresight to calculate the height of the city walls and to establish whether his scaling ladders were high enough.[93]

Until relatively recent years, mathematical and even relatively straightforward numerical materials relevant to decision making ran the risk of meeting with resistance, or of being ignored or misunderstood because of the decision-maker's inability to absorb such materials. One of Lord Cherwell's talents was his ability to present numerical materials and modes of calculation so that they would be "suitable to the comprehension of the Prime Minister."[94] There is no doubt today concerning the importance of sophisticated mathematical and statistical devices and numerical data in the preparation of briefs to be transformed into decisions. What is less clear is whether those responsible for making decisions are as yet more able to understand and absorb them than their predecessors of a

---

[89]Shang, p. 205.
[90]Ibid., pp. 218 and 318.
[91]Han Fei Tzu, cited in Shang, p. 218.
[92]Shang, p. 318.
[93]Polybius, vol. 1, p. 445.
[94]Birkenhead, p. 260.

generation or two ago. Still, the lengthy debates that revolve in the political sphere around statistical arguments and numerical data suggest that an educational process is under way.

The Intuitive Mind

In contrasting the intuitive with the mathematical mind, Pascal stressed the difficulty of achieving an arrangement of elements conducive to clear reasoning. Secondly, he emphasized the large number of principles or elements on which the intuitive mind operates. "These principles are so fine and so numerous that a very delicate and very clear sense is needed to perceive them." Since they do not lend themselves to a particularly orderly arrangement, "we must see the matter . . . at one glance, and not by a process of reasoning, at least to a certain degree." Because the host of intricately related elements do not lend themselves to clear isolation, arrangement, or limitation in numbers, "there is the greatest difficulty in making them felt by those who do not of themselves perceive them," that is, by those who possess the mathematical mind. The intuitive mind, on the contrary, while at home with such materials is totally taken aback when asked to work through the definitions, axioms and principles—which they find sterile and repellent—that the mathematical mind prefers.[95]

It is, presumably, intuition that enables some students of philosophy to derive, as Aristotle points out, conclusions that are more believable than the premises from which they are drawn.[96] Louis XIV was apparently speaking of the intuitive mind when he said that the function of a king consists principally in allowing good sense to act "which always acts naturally and without effort."[97] Franklin D. Roosevelt, we are told, worked "by apprehending through intuition a vast constellation of political forces. His complex administrative sensibility, infinitely subtle and sensitive, was forever

---

[95]Pascal, p. 2.

[96]Aristotle, *Rhetoric*, bk. III, 1418[a]. Sir Thomas Browne took the opposite view—the premises that men employ are more likely to be correct than the conclusions they draw from them. *Religio Medici*, p. 403.

[97]Louis XIV, p. 50.

weighing questions of personal force, of political timing, of congressional concern, of partisan benefit, of public interest. Situations had to be permitted to develop, to crystallize, to clarify . . . only then, at the long, frazzled end, would the President's intuitions consolidate and precipitate a result."[98]

While intuition has sometimes been viewed as a product of divine revelation, and sometimes as a mysterious faculty the source of whose success is unknown, others base the operation of the intuitive mind on the accumulation of experience. Experience also provides the limited number of premises on which the analytical or mathematical mind operates. But when experience is praised as a source of wisdom it is rather because of its provision of many inputs which are not even fully conscious in the intuitive mind but which nonetheless exercise a profound effect on its judgments. Commynes and Botero both emphasized experience as the most important source of political wisdom, but both were also agreed that purely personal experience was limited and required the extension that a knowledge of history provided. This knowledge was not the systematizing, generalizing knowledge sought by Machiavelli but rather simply an extension of personal experience. Even a man of no great learning could have as good judgment as learned men, provided he had sufficient experience.[99] Aristotle thought that what was true of medicine and law was also true of politics. Medical books are useful to experienced people rather than to the inexperienced, and works on constitutional and legal affairs are of little help to those without practice and experience.[100]

Most writers who emphasized the importance of experience did so without either insisting on the need to reduce it to explicit generalizations or to amplify it with the experience provided by history. Guicciardini is categorical that anyone who has exercised reponsibility will admit that experience accounts for many successes that native gifts could never provide.[101] Bacon, expressing what seems to be a sincere conviction on the importance of experience while at the same time paying a compliment to James I, noted that

---

[98]Schlesinger, 1959, p. 528.

[99]Botero, p. 51. See also Meinecke, p. 166.

[100]Aristotle, *Nichomachean Ethics*, bk. X, 1181^b.

[101]Guicciardini, *Maxims*, p. 43.

even a stick that had had the benefit of both long experience and eighteen years of conversation with the king would be turned into a statesman. Metternich whose many years of experience probably inclined him to attribute much to experience wrote that an intelligent man can make up for the lack of everything except experience.[102] Some six years later, writing to his son, Metternich referred to his irreplaceability and added, "To be what I am needs an accumulation of experience, and one could as easily replace an old tree as an old Minister."[103] And some eight years later Metternich explained his advantage over the genius of Thiers by the fact that he had been leader of the Austrian cabinet for twenty-eight years whereas Thiers was France's twenty-eighth foreign minister in the same period of time.[104] Another equally long-lived statesman, Konrad Adenauer, noted that a long life provides a greater opportunity to acquire experience. "Experience can be a guide to thought and action which nothing can replace, not even innate intellect. This is particularly true in the field of politics."[105]

Experience becomes a particularly important asset in the case of advisers operating in an unfamiliar environment and in applied areas that extend well beyond professional training. Scientists called to Washington have been particularly impressed by the importance of experience and "on-the-job training."[106]

Just as experience may provide premises for the mathematical mind but is generally viewed as primarily providing the multitudinous details and elements that provision the intuitive mind, so scholarship has a similar dual relationship to the mathematical and to the intuitive mind. Scholarship, however, as conceived by most of our writers is not the type of intellectual inquiry in which the mathematical mind shines. It is, rather, a broad, humanistic knowledge that contains historical learning, and philosophical and literary appreciation ranging from the classics to the present day. It may be said to include linguistic abilities the better to absorb man's written records and thus to increase sensitivity to the nuances of human experience, behavior, and thought. Learning, in this sense,

---

[102]Kissinger, 1957, p. 312.
[103]Sauvigny, p. 15.
[104]Ibid., p. 17.
[105]Adenauer, p. 15.
[106]Eiduson, p. 30.

is more a pleasure and prerequisite of the intuitive than of the mathematical mind. We shall see shortly, that such scholarship does not mean the pedantry often attributed to the professor. It is rather a learning whose best examples were often found outside the ranks of professional teachers and scholars. "Our nation's first great politicians," President Kennedy wrote, "—those who presided at its birth in 1776 and at its christening in 1787—included among their ranks most of the nation's first great writers and scholars."[107]

The intuitive mind, if freed from the desire or need to calculate, may become opportunistic. When Julian the Apostate urged his soldiers to join in seizing the "utmost bounds of Dacia" and wait until then to see "what ought further to be done," he was expressing the characteristic attitude of the opportunist rather than that of the careful planner or the analyst.[108] Oliver Cromwell provided what may be taken as the motto of the opportunist: A man never mounts higher than when he knows not whither he is going.[109] And this is echoed by Napoleon's much quoted "On s'engage et puis . . . on voit."

The Analytic and the Intuitive Mind in Politics

The characterizations of the analytic and the intuitive minds imply, when they do not already explicitly convey, not only a contrast of the one with the other but often an opposition or conflict between them. This conflict has existed through the ages, although it took on different nuances at different times and in different cultures. Generally, though, it has involved preferences for one of the poles in such dichotomies as Mind versus Heart, Rational versus Traditional, Moderns versus Ancients, Reason versus Intuition, Calculation versus Judgment, Scholar versus Actor, Theory versus Practice and Experience, Book Learning versus Common Sense.

These terms can be and have been arranged in different couplets, thus implying a certain unity among the terms of each side of the

---

[107]Cited in Schlesinger, 1965, p. 109.
[108]Marcellinus, *Julian the Apostate*, bk. 12.
[109]Adam Ferguson, p. 203.

opposition. The 'scholar,' however, has a somewhat ambiguous status; he is, in some forms, just as likely to be rejected by the intuitive and practical man as by the theoretician or calculator.

In feudal China the contrast was drawn more especially between the rational, legalist mind with its confidence in law, administrative efficiency, and calculation and its contempt for 'talkers' on the one hand, and the Confucian, on the other hand, with his emphasis on the wisdom of the sage who has incorporated that of past ages, a wisdom squarely based on moral and ritual standards. Occasionally, a contrast was drawn in a more modern spirit, namely between dependence on rules or recipes and reliance on a quick intelligence or cleverness, that is, between rational calculation and the nimbleness of intuition.[110]

Greek thought contrasted politics as a subject for study with politics as an art to be learned by practice and experience, the contrast being drawn very largely to the advantage of experience over booklearning and study. In Kautilya, too, we read that a man possessed of only theoretical knowledge and without practical experience is likely to commit serious blunders.[111]

In the Middle Ages, the numerous Mirrors of Kings, being themselves books written by scholars, gave prominence to the value of instruction derived from books while continuing to emphasize the indisputable value of the advice of old and therefore experienced counselors. The Mirrors of Kings thus tended to bring study and theory into a complementary rather than an antagonistic relation with experience—both sides of this dichotomy being areas in which many of their authors felt themselves fully able to make a positive contribution.[112]

In the Renaissance, theory and the rational mind were less concerned with the general study of government and the duties of the prince and more with the art of political calculation. Calculation was then contrasted with experience, both personal and that de-

---

[110]See Lie tseu, *Le Vrai Classique . . .*, p. 188.

[111]Shamasastry, *Kautilya's Arthasastra*, p. 13.

[112]In many societies, the least bookish of practical men is the merchant, but already in the thirteenth century in Norway, *The King's Mirror* was recommending to young men preparing for a merchant's career the study of arithmetic and law books: "Those who gain knowledge from books have keener wits than others." *The King's Mirror*, p. 81.

rived through historical study. Machiavelli, Guicciardini, and Botero were not especially concerned to express preferences for or opposition to one or the other term of this dichotomy, but rather were interested in their respective limitations.

In the seventeenth century, the discoveries and writings of Descartes, Newton, Locke, and others generated enormous enthusiasm and lent greatly increased value to man's analytic powers, with a corresponding depreciation, especially by Descartes, of historical study. While it is doubtful that the rationalist enthusiasm of scholars and intellectuals deeply affected the practice of politics by rulers and their advisers, the effect on discussions of the political art was clear. "The skill of making and maintaining commonwealths," wrote Hobbes, "consisteth in certain Rules, as doth Arithmetique and Geometry; not (as tennis play) on practise only."[113]

Descartes' disparagement of history did not go unchallenged. Pascal's judicious balancing of the virtues and limitations of both the mathematical and the intuitive minds already indicates a more restrained view. Vico, early in the eighteenth century, provided vigorous criticism of the pursuit of eternal truths so dear to the geometrician, and gave renewed attention to history and ancillary disciplines such as the study of mythology and linguistics.

The eighteenth and early nineteenth centuries saw in science, in philosophy, and in political and social revolutions developments sufficient to fortify rationalist aspirations, but these years also saw an emphasis on "silently working forces," on "the creativeness of long stretches of time" and on similar observations that tended to view politics as a function of a sensitive awareness of man's place in a slow stream of development. "The science of constructing a commonwealth or renovating it or reforming it," wrote Edmund Burke, "is, like every other experimental science, not to be taught *a priori*. Nor is it a short experience that can instruct us in that practical science."[114] And in Germany, Adam Müller proclaimed: "The constitution of states cannot be invented; the cleverest calculation in this matter is as futile as total ignorance."[115]

---

[113]Hobbes, p. xii.

[114]Burke, in a letter to C. J. Fox, nonetheless wrote, " . . . though I am sensible that those who are best provided with a general scheme, are fittest to take advantage of all contingencies." Edmund Burke to C. J. Fox, October 8, 1777.

[115]Cited in Mannheim, p. 210. Adam Müller's statement is taken by Mannheim as

In the contemporary period the contest between the analytic and intuitive minds has been, perhaps, sharper than at any previous time. This arose from the extraordinary development on the analytic side of disciplines, devices and organizations dedicated to the fullest exploitation of the rational powers of the human mind. Mathematical disciplines no longer remained—as they had been previously—largely an inspiration toward a certain outlook that had relatively little effect on day-to-day politics. Mathematics and statistics, game theory and decision theory, military and political gaming, simulation, cost-benefit analysis and program budgeting, organization theory, econometric and other areas of mathematical modeling, operations research, management science, policy science, psephology (the 'science' of polling), theoretical developments in the social sciences generally, and quantification on a grand scale did not remain confined to academic and business circles but achieved substantial success in claiming the attention of political and administrative leaders. Important supporting developments took place in computer technology and in the growth of organizations for the development and exploitation of these intellectual developments. Professional organizations, professional schools, and institutes for the training of policy analysts have developed on a substantial scale and given an increased impetus to the application of the new methods and disciplines in virtually all spheres of government and corporate life. On the other side, intuition naturally enough remained simply intuition; the claims of practical experience, historical knowledge, and political 'sensitivity' were hardly capable of developing greater importance or new dimensions. Perhaps the output of the experienced, well-stocked, and well-disciplined mind may have been improved by the increased demands in the contemporary period for rigor and clarity. But these are qualities that are equally absent in the poorer specimens of both the analytic and intuitive minds and equally present in the better specimens of both.

The rival claims of analysis and intuition (experience) produced considerable debate concerning the limitations of each. Convictions

---

a characteristic idea and leading theme of the early nineteenth-century conservative tradition. The same idea can, as a matter of fact, be found in similar language in a very different political climate, Adam Ferguson (1768), p. 204.

concerning the unpredictability of the future and the great role that luck and chance play in history implied that planning and calculation have strict limits imposed upon them. For Aristotle, goodness, wealth, physical endowment, and other virtues were not sufficient to ensure happiness. To make life really secure, a measure of luck is required.[116] The role of luck and chance was no less marked in politics. Chance and Fortune had their goddess, Tyche, daughter of Zeus, who appropriately enough juggles a ball to exemplify the uncertainties of life, just as Nemesis, her Latin counterpart, has her wheel. Boethius, following Aristotle, defined Chance in a form particularly relevant to those engaged in political pursuits: "Whenever anything is done with one intention, but something else, other than was intended, results . . . that is called chance."[117]

Polybius' history of the rise of the Roman Empire was written, he tells us, to show how the normal working of cause and effect is upset by the caprices of good or bad Fortune. Polybius wanted his work to teach men how to bear the vicissitudes of Fortune. But he stressed, as did Machiavelli and Guicciardini, that these vicissitudes may spell opportunity, as it did when a Carthaginian war vessel accidentally—that is unpredictably—fell into Roman hands. The Romans seized on this model to build a fleet of their own that they developed with extreme speed, training oarsmen ashore on mock-ups of the vessels pending their completion.[118] Polybius would agree with the Athenian Stranger in Plato's *Laws* that man never legislates but rather accidents of all sorts legislate for him.[119]

Demosthenes condemned the inclination to calculate at a time when what was called for was courageous action: "Soldiers and comrades . . . I hope that none of you in our present strait will think to show his wit by exactly calculating all the perils that encompass us, but that you will rather hasten to close with the enemy, without staying to count the odds. . . . In emergencies like ours calculation is out of place."[120]

---

[116]Aristotle, *Rhetoric*, bk. I, 1360[b].
[117]Boethius, p. 102.
[118]Polybius, vol. 1, p. 23.
[119]Plato, *Laws*, bk. IV(709).
[120]Thucydides, p. 213.

Commynes showed no great confidence in military planning. "I think," he wrote, "no man's wisdom can guide or give order to such a great number of men and that things in the field seldom turn out as they have been planned indoors."[121] For Commynes, Fortune was less a Greek goddess and more the Christian God arranging things beyond the understanding of man.[122] The great turning point in the fortunes of the Duke of Burgundy, Commynes' first master, came when the Duke's advance guard, prior to a battle, decided to join up with the main force. The latter, thinking that the vanguard was taking flight, themselves took flight. Word of the Duke's defeat spread rapidly, led to the defection of one ally after another, so that in a short space of time his position was totally altered, all this as a result of the action of the vanguard or rather the misinterpretation that was made of it.[123] Commynes and other writers take considerable delight in emphasizing these sudden changes in the fortunes of great men and in demonstrating the inability of calculation to forestall them. It was for this reason that Guicciardini considered it "madness" to relinquish a certain good to avoid an uncertain evil, unless that evil was very great.[124]

Because the power of *Fortuna* was so great it was incumbent upon political planners to have alternate plans. Guicciardini, however, was not convinced that this would do much good, particularly in dealing with an enemy. The enemy, inspired by the position he is in, will generally think of something that will not occur to his antagonist.[125] Guicciardini recommended to statesmen to rely not on knowledge of historical patterns but rather on their knowledge

[121]Commynes, p. 73.

[122]The identification of *Fortuna* with God was not uncommon although it is difficult to know how much of this was an attempt to avoid trouble with the Church. The Church viewed notions such as fate as a pagan residue, and the Inquisition forbade the use of the word *fata*. One author having need of the word *fata* printed it *facta*, but in the errata entered "For *facta*, read *fata*." When Montaigne showed the manuscript of his *Essays* in Rome, his attention was drawn to the fact that he had used the word fortune. Montaigne had considerable respect for *Fortuna* and the limitations it imposed on deliberation and planning. Montaigne, vol. 1, p. 170.

[123]Commynes, p. 280.

[124]Guicciardini, *Maxims*, p. 47.

[125]Ibid., p. 83.

of men, from which they might be able to deduce guidance for political action.[126]

Botero recommended that the leader avoid planning actions in detail and allow developing circumstances to dictate the subsequent stages of action.[127]

Machiavelli was not at all disposed to underestimate the role of the purely accidental in political action and the dangers that this imposed. But he took a less pessimistic view and held that man's will and ingenuity, his *virtù*, that is, his strength of character and drive, could do much to mitigate his dependence on *Fortuna*.[128] Even Guicciardini, despite all his qualifications, acknowledged that a wise man must, after all, rely on reason.[129]

In France, Budé showed considerable individuality in emphasizing the role of economic riches in determining the fate of nations, and relegated *Fortuna* to a secondary role. For Budé, *Fortuna* played a role primarily in those areas of life such as war, which men ought, in any case, to avoid.[130] Louis XIV was not disposed to accept this: "Wisdom directs that on certain occasions we allow much to chance. In such cases reason herself counsels us to follow some kind of blind motion. . . . No one can say when we should distrust or obey this motion; neither books, nor rules, nor experience tell us; a certain appropriateness, a certain daring of the mind . . . enables us to discover this."[131] And Frederick the Great acknowledged to Voltaire that "the older one becomes, the more one is persuaded that His Sacred Majesty Chance does three-quarters of the work of this miserable Universe."[132]

---

[126]Hale, p. xxvi.

[127]Botero, p. 46.

[128]In addition to *ragione, Fortuna,* and *virtù*, the statesmen and political thinkers of the Italian Renaissance recognized the operation of *Necessità. Fortuna* left room to the statesman for maneuver, but there are situations where a stern necessity permits absolutely no choice and there is nothing to do except to bow to it. It was *Necessità* of which Metternich spoke when he wrote, "There are times in the affairs of men when the strongest will, the most legitimate resistance, is broken against an imperious necessity to which everything must submit." Sauvigny, p. 82.

[129]Guicciardini, *Maxims*, p. 75.

[130]Budé, pp. 56–58.

[131]Louis XIV, p. 65.

[132]Cited in Spengler, vol. 1, p. 142.

In the modern period, preoccupation with *Fortuna* and its role in the affairs of men has declined. Meinecke saw in Ranke's conception of history failure to allow for the influence of chance or accident on the course of events.[133] Meinecke's criticism does not seem to have greatly influenced modern conceptions of the historical process. President Kennedy, we are told, had an embarrassed confidence in his luck, but this was an individual sentiment and not a principled view of the political process.[134] Truman's statement that "any school boy's afterthought is worth more than the forethought of the greatest statesman" reflects a more serious view of the nature of political history.[135]

Views in the spirit of the French and Italian Renaissance still survive. Hans Morgenthau writes: "The luck of the statesman is the luck of the speculator rather than of the gambler. It means to be attuned in a mysterious way to the objective situation. . . . That is roughly what Bismarck meant when . . . he wrote that the best the statesman can do is to listen to the footsteps of God striding through history and try to grasp the hem of his vestment when he walks by. . . . The Statesman . . . must behold himself not as the infallible arbiter of the destiny of men, but as the handmaiden of something which he may use but cannot control. *Fortuna* smiles only on those who concede her the last word."[136]

It would be a mistake to suppose that the representatives of the mathematical or analytical mind have failed to take account of the role of chance and the difficulties this places in the path of rational calculation and planning. Much of contemporary decision-making theory and of the statistical and mathematical techniques associated with it and with related disciplines (see page 144 above) are based on a sophisticated probabilistic treatment of uncertainties and ignorance and is precisely intended, in the service of rationality, to tame and subdue *Fortuna*. The Renaissance also acknowledged the need to grapple with the goddess; but in that period *Fortuna* was in considerable measure to be tamed by the *virtù* of the leader, that is, by his strength of will and by his ability to create opportunities out of

[133]Meinecke, p. xxxv.
[134]Schlesinger, 1965, p. 214.
[135]Truman, vol. 2, p. x.
[136]Morgenthau, p. 61.

the hazards of the unpredictable. Despite this activistic attitude, Renaissance statesmen and historians retained a profound sense of the incalculable; it is this deep sentiment that seems largely absent from contemporary representatives of the analytic mind. This is understandable since the powerful instruments at their disposal have perhaps given them a too-confident sense that man's cunning enables him to skirt the traps set by Tyche and Nemesis.

In addition to the problems created for the theoretical or analytical mind by the unpredictable are those that stem from the difficulties and dangers resulting from basing political behavior on simplified generalizations. Aristotle had said: "In practical life, particular facts count more than generalizations."[137] Some six hundred years ago Ibn Khaldun discussed the relevance of generalizations and abstractions in terms that a statesman or historian could hardly improve on today. "Scholars are of all men those least fitted for politics and its ways. The reason for this is that they are accustomed to intellectual speculation, the search for concepts. . . . All these operations aim at attaining the universal aspect of things, not those particular to . . . a person, generation, nation, or particular class of men. They then seek to apply these universal concepts. . . . Those who engage in politics must pay great attention . . . to all the circumstances that accompany and succeed an event. For politics are tortuous and may contain elements which prevent the subsumption of a given event under a universal concept or maxim. . . . Hence men of learning, who are accustomed to generalizations . . . tend, when dealing with political affairs, to impose their own framework of concepts . . . thus falling into error. . . . The ordinary sound man of average intelligence, however, whose mind is unaccustomed to such speculation . . ., judges each case on its own merits and every category of men or of things according to its own peculiarities. . . ."[138]

Guicciardini was equally convinced that it was quite impossible to generalize and speak "by the book." The distinctions and exceptions that characterize individual cases cannot be covered by a single general rule. "They must be taught by discretion."[139]

---

[137]Aristotle, *Rhetoric*, bk. II, 1393[a].

[138]Issawi, pp. 64–66.

[139]Guicciardini, *Maxims*, p. 42.

Again, "Every tiny, particular circumstance that changes is apt to alter a conclusion. The affairs of this world, therefore, cannot be judged from afar but must be judged and resolved day by day."[140]

Pascal whose mathematical discoveries and *Pensées* entitle him to speak for both the mathematical and the intuitive minds also emphasized that in the world of action the omission of a single element may lead to error and that it requires the global perception of the intuitive mind to grasp all the relevant elements at once and to avoid drawing false deductions from them. Mathematicians who try to deal mathematically with matters requiring the *esprit de finesse* "make themselves ridiculous, wishing to begin with definitions and then with axioms, which is not the way to proceed in this kind of reasoning." Mathematicians who are only mathematicians, continued Pascal, have exact minds only if everything is explained to them by definitions and axioms. "Otherwise they are inaccurate and insufferable."[141] Guicciardini has a thought related to Pascal's point. If someone has poor judgment, it is much better to let him deal in generalities because if you show him all the details he simply becomes confused.[142] The generalities, however, may not be of much use. Henry Kissinger, speaking of the utilization of intellectuals in government work, refers to one segment of them who work on abstract models which it is impossible to make relevant for policy action.[143]

Criticism of the *esprit de géométrie* may derive not so much from the intellectual limitations of theory and mensuration but rather from a moral indifference or obtuseness sometimes attributed, probably unjustly, to the specialist in abstractions. Seneca's outburst against the geometrician is by no means peculiar to his place and time.[144]

---

[140]Ibid., p. 70.

[141]Pascal, pp. 1–2.

[142]Guicciardini, *Maxims*, p. 80.

[143]Kissinger, 1974, p. 642.

[144]"The geometrician teaches me how to work out the size of my estates—rather than how to work out how much a man needs in order to have enough. . . . What use is it to me to be able to divide a piece of land into equal areas if I'm unable to divide it with a brother? What use is the ability to measure out a portion of an acre with an accuracy extending even to the bits which elude the measuring rod if I'm upset when some high-handed neighbor encroaches slightly on my property? . . . Oh, the marvels of geometry! You geometers can calculate the

The criticisms of or limitations imputed to theory, reason, and measurement did not go unanswered. Montaigne had no great confidence in practical experience. He acknowledged that where reason and knowledge were lacking we are led to employ experience. But experience, nonetheless, is a "much feebler and lower means."[145]

The considerable difficulty of attaching to the term intuition a precise account of the attributes and processes intended by the word and the unfortunate tendency to describe it as a "mysterious" faculty (see, for example, Morgenthau, p. 148 above) make it an easy target for attack. Nonetheless, such attacks have to be conducted with discretion since mathematicians, scientists, and philosophers with the greatest confidence in rationality nonetheless also call upon intuition, imagination, insight, creativity as necessary supplementary talents or skills capable of reaching conclusions just as valid as those attained by the theoretical mind. Unfortunately, the *esprit de finesse* is often incapable of establishing demonstrations able to convince those whose perceptions have not led them to the same conclusion.

The practitioners of theory are no doubt also correct in charging that their critics often have an unhealthy suspicion of what they themselves cannot do and fear that the value of their own special skills is being undermined. Opposition to what is new and plain ignorance of what the theoretical and quantitative mind is up to also sometimes lead to sterile criticism. In any event, the issue here is not the respective capabilities or merits of the theoretical and intuitive mind in the pursuit of scientific knowledge, but rather in the application of mind to the tasks and decisions of political life. In this area, it is probably true that in the contemporary period the development of analytic procedures and the mode of education they have given rise to have made it more difficult for the proponents of 'calculation' and 'wisdom' to understand each other to the degree that was possible in past ages.

Bacon recognized in his day that the reduction of political wisdom

---

areas of circles, can reduce any given shape to a square, can state the distances separating stars. . . . Well, if you're such an expert, measure a man's soul; tell me how large or how small that is. You can define a straight line; what use is that to you if you've no idea what straightness means in life?" Seneca, pp. 153–154.

[145]Montaigne, vol. 4, p. 290.

or business acumen to rules or prescriptions that could be transmitted by books, that is, by education rather than by prolonged experience, had not yet been made. But he viewed the effort as eminently worthwhile and, it would seem, capable of success: "The wisdom touching Negotiation or Business hath not been hitherto collected into writing, to the great derogation of learning and the professors of learning. For from this root springeth chiefly that note or opinion, which by us is expressed in adage to this effect, that there is no great concurrence between learning and wisdom. . . . For if books were written of this [negotiation, business, politics] . . . I doubt not but learned men with mean experience would far excel men of long experience without learning, and outshoot them in their own bow."[146] The last sentence is striking in its affirmation that the reduction of experience and practice to written formulations would permit the person of little practical experience to excel those of long experience but limited learning. It is, of course, confidence that this reduction has been achieved that encourages today the growth of centers where persons of little or no experience in "Negotiation" or "Business" may learn to "outshoot" experienced managers and practitioners with "their own bow." It is an open question whether most texts used in public policy and management programs answer to the type of books that Bacon had in mind, or whether they avoid the pitfalls of excessive abstraction noted by Ibn Khaldun, or whether, in short, they have indeed provided that "concurrence between learning and wisdom" that Bacon so earnestly desired.

The Managers

The word 'expert' is derived, via Old French, from the Latin *expertus* signifying "tried," that is, "arising out of practice or experience or experiment." It is characteristic of the development of specialized knowledge that today the expert is characterized less by his experience than by his education and degrees, that is, by his book and school training. In many fields experience is an additional, but not basic, qualification of the expert. This higher degree of training

[146]Bacon, "Advancement of Learning," *Selected Writings*, pp. 347–348.

and professionalization has favored the development of a guild or corporate spirit among experts and sets them off more sharply from the man of common sense than was the case when the expert was primarily a man of practical experience.

The contemporary expert is very much a committee man, much of whose work is performed in meetings with his colleagues or in other forms of collaborative effort. He often has operational and administrative responsibilities, particularly when he is part of a government or business organization. Committee meetings often stimulate critical rather than creative faculties so that their deliberations readily revolve around hazards, drawbacks, and other reasons for rejecting various lines of action rather than around the creation of policy. To the extent that the expert and his colleagues are embedded in a bureaucracy they are also tempted to search for administrative solutions to problems. A principal feature of bureaucracies is a striving for safety and calculability, and this induces a tendency to avoid the uncertainties and risks generally inherent in new policies. In foreign affairs, "the concern with technical problems . . . leads to a standard which evaluates by mistakes avoided rather than by goals achieved, and to a belief that ability is more likely to be judged by the pre-vision of catastrophes than the discovery of opportunities."[147] When the substantive expert is not himself turned into a bureaucrat and manager, he sometimes finds that he is being displaced or controlled by those whose expertise lies largely in managerial or organizational skills. In 1970 the State Department of the United States instituted reforms that suggested a considerable enhancement of the influence of the managers. The Department "has relied too long on the 'generalist' and has been slow to recruit and develop officers in the wide range of special aptitudes, skills, and knowledge which the new diplomacy requires." What the new diplomacy requires, it seems, is "a new breed of diplomat-managers, just as able as the best of the old school, but equipped with up-to-date techniques and backed by a Department organized on modern management principles."[148] These "up-to-date techniques" have, in fact, not demonstrated their superior relevance for the tasks of United States foreign policy.

---

[147]Kissinger, 1957, p. 327.
[148]*Diplomacy for the Seventies*, pp. 4–5.

Characteristically, the 1970 reform focused less on substantive foreign policy issues than on improving management skills and devising procedures for the study of issues, devising procedures being, no doubt, a more congenial object of attention than the issues themselves.[149] Dean Acheson, reacting against this displacement of attention, exaggerated, very usefully, a point that the managers often do not care to acknowledge. "Good men can run the worst kind of organization and poor men can't run the best."[150]

The managers and the bureaucratized experts are sometimes excessively appreciative of motion and activity, "Momentum is confused with purpose."[151] The emphasis on administrative action is all the more understandable when the expert is chosen, as he frequently is, not for his substantive knowledge but for his administrative talent. It is understandable that he may be inclined to meet issues by taking administrative actions, since otherwise his alienation from substantive matters might lead him into conflict with experts able to take issue with him.

The manager-expert and the expert are characterized at times by a certain presumptuousness that derives from a conviction that modern administrative and intellectual techniques permit them to act in a variety of fields in which they not only have limited knowledge and experience but are even too ignorant or unpractised to be sensitive to the gaps in their capabilities. Jonathan Swift, writing of the political disputations of the technical experts in Laputa, added "I have indeed observed the same disposition among most of the mathematicians I have known in Europe, although I could never discover the least analogy between the two sciences; unless those people suppose, that because the smallest circle hath as many degrees as the largest, therefore the regulation and management of the world require no more abilities than the handling and turning of a globe."[152] Edmund Burke rebuked those not foolish enough to meddle with a clock yet confident that they know how to take to pieces and put together social machinery. "Men little think how immorally they act in rashly meddling with what they do not un-

---

[149]Goldhamer, p. 263.
[150]*Los Angeles Times*, December 13, 1970.
[151]Kissinger, 1960, p. 344.
[152]Swift, p. 192.

derstand." Many manager-experts are not overly endowed with that sense of the intricacies and complexities of the world that a sage will freely acknowledge.[153] The Taoists had a profound sense of how often the attempt to do good results in evil.[154] Such convictions can lead to paralysis and quietism, but the absence of any distrust of man's ability to do good encourages a misleading optimism and brashness.

Accounts of the early days of the Kennedy Administration reveal a confidence and enthusiasm that was little justified. "The excitement in the White House infected the whole Executive Branch. A new breed had come to town, and the New Frontiersmen carried a thrust of action and purpose wherever they went."[155] Later, at a news conference, President Kennedy described himself as "depressed," a word rare in his vocabulary. "The Alliance for Progress," he said, "has failed to some degree because the problems are almost insuperable."[156] Clearly, "the thrust of action and purpose" had provided expectations that were unreal. During the "dramatic beginnings" of the Alliance for Progress and the Peace Corps "euphoria reigned; we thought for a moment that the world was plastic and the future unlimited."[157] This characteristic attitude of the managers, of the organizational men, and of the expert working in an unfamiliar area generally brings its own swift punishment. Schlesinger, embarrassed by his acknowledgement of "plastic worlds" and "unlimited futures," added: "Yet I don't suppose we really thought this. At bottom we knew how intractable the world was."[158] But did they? Perhaps it was President Truman's close reading of history that led him, on the contrary, to characterize as thoroughly American the tendency to believe that any problem can be solved with a little ingenuity and without much inconvenience.[159]

A large measure of confidence is especially characteristic of scientists, who as a group have been future oriented and optimistic.

---

[153]*Comprehensive Discussions in the White Tiger Hall*, vol. 2, p. 523.
[154]Waley, pp. 102, 103, and 110.
[155]Schlesinger, 1965, p. 210.
[156]Sorenson, 1965, p. 535.
[157]Schlesinger, 1965, p. 214.
[158]Ibid.
[159]Miller, p. 240.

The optimism justified in scientific and engineering fields spills over into social planning and social administration. It is not always appreciated in some government and professional circles that the skills that made the Apollo mission a reasonable undertaking did not indicate the availability of knowledge relevant for economic and political 'engineering.' A more advanced state of knowledge in the social disciplines would not, in any case, have altered the situation greatly, since an essential difference between physical and social engineering is not their relative state of knowledge but the nature of the materials worked on, a difference sometimes ignored. The 'hostile' environment of outer space was, in fact, neutral and indifferent, characteristics that scarcely describe any social environment. "He who would scheme and project for others, will find an opponent in every person who is disposed to scheme for himself."[160] When difficulties arise and failures occur, these often suggest to the managerial temperament not certain limitations imposed by the nature of the social-political reality, but rather failure along remediable, often administrative, dimensions. Not the principal goals nor the basic understanding of the situation but rather the particular means employed are subjected to review.

A high regard for administrative devices and technical knowledge induces a neglect of the role of leadership in political planning and program implementation. In earlier centuries in which authority was more frequently centered in a few individuals, the quality of leadership was of great importance, and this was vividly evident to historians, to political analysts, and to political leaders themselves. Whether as the Prophet, the Hero, or the possessor of *virtù* or charisma,[161] the leader was recognized not by whether he held the top job but by whether he possessed the drive, the courage, the character, the creativity, and the ability to inspire by word,

---

[160]Adam Ferguson, pp. 202–203.

[161]*Virtù* is the Renaissance Italian equivalent of charisma. Both terms refer to certain extraordinary qualities of some individuals that give them leadership in political, religious, moral, or military roles. For Machiavelli and writers of his period, *virtù* represented qualities of energy, courage, indomitable will, a capacity to inspire loyalty and devotion that enabled their possessors to overcome the hazards represented by *Fortuna* and to seize the opportunities she affords. Max Weber emphasized the innovative aspect of the charismatic leader who destroys the existing bases of authority and attaches it to his own person. See Weber, pp. 358–392.

gesture, or bearing the respect or devotion that enabled him to impose himself and his aims on others.

Democratic politics with its requirement for soliciting votes would seem to provide a competitive process in which *virtù* and charisma have an opportunity to outstrip the undistinguished and the commonplace. And certainly on many occasions they do. But the exigencies of party and convention politics, campaign financing and several other features of the political system considerably reduce the opportunity for *virtù* to assert itself, even when it exists and might be disposed to enter the political lists.

The reliance on organization and technique often obscures to the managers and the experts the nature and significance of leadership, but not so completely as to make them indifferent to its relation to voting. In conformity with the application of administrative and organizational remedies for substantive problems, a facsimile of leadership is manufactured. Eric Sevareid referred to this process when he spoke of the Nixon and Kennedy campaigns: "The 'managerial revolution' has come to politics and Nixon and Kennedy are its first completely packaged products." These "tidy, buttoned-down men" represented, according to Sevareid, not the heroic leader but the junior executive on the make and the apotheosis of the Organization Man.[162]

If the country wants leadership, the quantity of it can, it seems, be increased overnight. Robert T. Hartmann, counselor to President Ford, describing the president's half-dozen rehearsals before television cameras of an important public address, observed: "We'll know in a day or two whether the speech was a flop or a success. We'll learn whether he is demonstrating the leadership qualities everybody is demanding he demonstrate."[163] One might well suppose it is the function of an adviser to assist the president in making a favorable public appearance. But it is an interesting revelation of how far the political packaging process has gone that counselor Hartmann did not think it inappropriate to publicize the packaging process that went on behind the scenes. The careful staging of a public appearance by a political leader is understandable and by no means ridiculous. As General de Gaulle has pointed out, great

[162]Schlesinger, 1965, p. 64.
[163]*Los Angeles Times*, January 14, 1975.

leaders have always stage-managed their appearances to produce calculated effects and to impress their audiences.[164] But he took it for granted that the leader is endowed with a sense of presence that enables him to maintain the necessary presence himself rather than being manipulated like a mannequin in the hands of a window dresser. Experts in 'political consultancy' who gladly undertake such tasks now constitute a new profession sufficiently developed in the United States and some other countries to be organized into the International Association of Political Consultants.[165]

The products of political consultancy and the great range in leadership capabilities in the political world are phenomena of greater importance to policy planning, the policy analyst, and the political adviser than is generally recognized. Many types of policies and programs are viable and relevant only when introduced and implemented by an appropriate leadership. In many instances programs may conform to all other planning criteria but fail to take into account available leadership. Public acceptance may be weak and successful implementation impossible. "Public opinion is everything," said Lincoln. "With it nothing can fail, without it nothing can succeed." Failure may, of course, be due to nonacceptance by political leaders themselves, a point generally well recognized. Contemporary policy analysis also recognizes that recommendations have to take account of conflicting interest groups and have to be designed to circumvent the paralyzing effect of such clashes of interest. What is less commonly recognized, however, is that it is precisely a function of effective political leadership to dominate such conflicts and to produce a solution less influenced by extraneous power considerations. Where effective political leadership is absent or weak, program planning and implementation must necessarily pursue paths different from those relevant where the highest conditions of political leadership are fulfilled. For many objectives, policy analysis and program planning are the last things needed. What may be most needed is an effective political leader

---

[164]de Gaulle, pp. 58–59.

[165]These experts held their third annual meeting in London in 1970 but were not thereby successful in inducing any British representation, although delegates from fifteen other countries including the United States were present. *The Economist*, December 19, 1970, p. 28.

who will make the objective his own, after which program planning may become relevant. When Machiavelli pleaded for a united Italy in the famous last chapter of *The Prince*,[166] it was not an astute political design or program for this objective that he sought, but rather to inspire a leader to undertake the task. And it was not a particular political program but the emergence of leaders like Cavour and Garibaldi that did indeed finally fulfill Machiavelli's goal. Colonel House's objectives in the domestic sphere were also pursued not by trying to formulate and 'sell' a program, but by searching for a capable political leader to whom he could lend his support.[167] It is not the function or responsibility of the policy analyst to transform himself into a political talent scout or political manager, but it is a characteristic of contemporary policy analysis to disregard leadership requirements inherent in proposed programs, and after programs have failed, to seek in a revision of the program itself the success that eluded achievement.

The increased requirements for substantive knowledge, analytic skills, research, and large bodies of data have meant that the political leader often does not have sufficient substantive knowledge to work effectively with professionally equipped advisers. Partly as a result of this, it has become possible for academic and other professional persons not only to achieve important advisory posts but also public office.

Since book learning has more readily become a platform to advancement in practical politics than was generally the case in the past, attitudes toward the academic and the professional take on a new significance. The professor is no longer simply involved in the conflict of practical experience with theory, but also in conflicts for the rewards of power and influence. Professionals have found in the political sector a relatively new area which can provide economic benefits and the related satisfactions of prestige and influence. Thus the effects of professional self-confidence noted above are intensified by professional vested interests which, in their turn, have been reinforced in the United States by the magnitude of United States international and domestic activities that have come to employ important sectors of the professional community.

[166]Machiavelli, *The Prince*, pp. 94–98.
[167]House, vol. 1, p. 46.

The expert and the professor could hardly avoid reproaches of self-interest and professional aggrandizement in a period in which professional training provided so many opportunities. In addition, the scholar has not been able to shake, even during this period of enhanced importance, a reputation that Seneca had already provided almost two thousand years ago in describing the guardians of learning as "pedantic, irritating, tactless, self-satisfied bores."[168] It was, no doubt, a similar opinion that led Metternich to write "I could wish that for the good of humanity there could be learning but no learned men."[169] Metternich also noted, gratefully, that "there are no clumsier conspirators than professors, individually or in groups." The conservative statesmen's intemperate ridicule of the nineteenth-century academician—often a political liberal—is even more bluntly conveyed by Bismarck's remark that it made no difference what sort of person became chancellor provided he wasn't a professor.[170]

The development in recent years of a considerable superstructure of terminology in those social sciences eager to lay claim to scientific excellence has increased their reputation for enveloping ideas in impenetrable jargon. When Theodore Sorensen submitted his analysis of Democratic concern with the anti-Catholic vote in 1960 to a professor, he resented receiving advice that he should have referred to "situations in which Catholicism is an independent variable of fluctuating salience with respect to the voting choice."[171]

In democratic societies attitudes toward the managers, the experts, and the professors have sometimes been affected less by their alleged presumption or pedantry than by a fear that their near monopoly of knowledge and their employment in the political sector afford them a degree of power inconsistent with democratic aspirations. The technocratic or managerial revolution announced

[168]Seneca, p. 159.

[169]Metternich added: "Artists are much better value. They are usually a little queer in the head but their hearts are sound." Sauvigny, p. 60.

[170]von Bülow, vol. 3, pp. 171–172.

[171]Sorensen, 1965, p. 83. The reviewer, in a nonprofessional magazine, of a major American work on political science, cannot be reproached for describing as a smoke screen and word-magic passages such as: "At the level of basic attitudes there is largely an unconscious consensus of feelings with regard to values and of reactions regarded as suitable in response to certain political cues."

by Thorstein Veblen in 1919 in *The Engineers and the Price System*, and periodically reannounced by later writers, drew attention to the interposition of the expert between the ordinary citizen and government and to the transformation of public debate into technical directions that often debar the citizen from effective choice and therefore from participation in the political process. The expert may, of course, also be distrusted for pursuing scientific interests thought more likely to maim than to heal the social body.

The periodic distrust of the technocrat, the expert, and the professor has been aggravated from time to time by the suspicion that their political, moral, or religious loyalties are suspect. On the whole, however, the pluralism of most contemporary societies and the fragmentation of what were once more monolithic social classes, has prevented the expert or professional sector from becoming, over any prolonged period, a major target of public or governmental hostility. The scientists, the professors, and the experts in technical, commercial, industrial, and political fields, represent among themselves social elements stemming from and allied with a great diversity of sectors in the society, and this has provided a considerable measure of protection against any form of unremitting hostility.

Virtue

The adviser's first loyalty is normally to his prince, but we have seen that other loyalties—to a religion, an ideology, a political party, or the welfare of the people—may take precedence. Many advisers deserved well of those subject to the prince's authority. They opposed war, partly because of its riskiness but also because it imposed enormous costs on the people. "The only important point in military affairs," announced Hsüntze, "is in getting the accord of the people."[172]

Advisers and political writers showed surprising unanimity in emphasizing to their princes the importance of protecting the people both from his own exactions and those of the nobility. Occasionally the writers of the Mirrors of Kings and other manuals of statecraft based their plea on moral grounds, but mostly they ap-

---

[172]Hsüntze, p. 158.

pealed to its instrumental value, often clearly because a purely moral argument might not have carried much weight. Gilbert of Tournai, writing at the request of Louis IX, urged the prince to promote the welfare of his subjects because it was right to do so, but then added that it would also make the prince's position more secure.[173] Most writers, however, rested their case on expediency alone. Even Aquinas urged the king to cultivate the love of his people because it would provide an indispensable support for him; those who are kept down by fear will rebel when opportunity arises.[174] Joinville approvingly tells of a friar who preached before Louis IX that a kingdom had never been lost except where first there had been a failure of justice.[175] "Whoever loses the favor of his people," warned Erasmus, "is thereby stripped of a great safeguard."[176]

Commynes who, like Joinville, was an experienced counselor and not simply a writer of manuals repeatedly emphasized in his *Memoirs* the importance of treating the people with consideration. To be sure, the people to whom he mostly referred were those of high rank because, as he said, to deal with all the people of middling and small estate would take him too long,[177] a discrimination that would have astonished and probably horrified ancient Chinese political writers much of whose attention was precisely claimed by the common people. Commynes did reproach Louis for spending too much on fortification and other ambitious projects, and thereby taking from the poor to give to those who had no need of it. He also advised that when new lands were acquired, the inhabitants be treated better than they had been by their former masters.[178] These and similar views did not necessarily prevail in the councils of kings. But in any case, advisers were clearly far from always being cynical men who incited their masters to indulge their worst impulses, a charge that can be made more often against the princes' retainers and courtiers.

---

[173]Born, 1928a, pp. 479–480.
[174]Aquinas, pp. 45–47.
[175]Joinville, p. 149.
[176]Erasmus, pp. 13 and 209.
[177]Commynes, p. 348.
[178]Ibid., pp. 346 and 278.

Few advisers to the prince have had a worse reputation than Machiavelli, whose name has entered the language as a synonym for deceit, cunning, and callousness. But this Renaissance political analyst, in discussing the prince's treatment of the people, did not differ in any essential respect from those writers who preceded him. Machiavelli stressed the importance, in entering a province, of enlisting the support of the people, no matter how powerful the prince's army might be. The prince should not tamper with their institutions nor impose new taxes and unfamiliar laws. It is perfectly true that Machiavelli wrote that men must be either caressed or destroyed. Populations accustomed to liberty never forget their former privileges, and if the prince was not prepared to live among them and cultivate them, he would be compelled to destroy them. For Machiavelli, the proper choice was clearly "to caress" and not "to destroy." In ancient Rome the political leaders had to satisfy the army because the army was stronger than the people. But in our day, Machiavelli pointed out, the people are stronger than the army.[179] "The best fortress is to be found in the love of the people, for although you may have fortresses they will not save you if you are hated by the people."[180] Again, "it is necessary for a prince to possess the friendship of the people; otherwise he has no resource in times of adversity."[181] Machiavelli nonetheless showed some uncertainty concerning the relative merits of love and fear in providing security for the prince. In *The Prince* he wrote that both were necessary but fear was more certain. However, in a letter to his friend Soderini, he pondered the meaning of examples from Roman history that showed that both cruelty and humanity had in different cases successfully served the same end.[182] Machiavelli not only had a high regard for the power of the people, but he also held an opinion concerning them that we tend to associate with a later period of political development: the people, he said, have better judgment than a prince, and when they are given an opportunity to choose, they usually discern the truth and make the right de-

[179]Machiavelli, *The Prince*, pp. 6–9, 18–19, and 75–76.
[180]Ibid., p. 81.
[181]Ibid., p. 38.
[182]Machiavelli, "Choix de lettres," in *Le Prince*, pp. 277–278.

cision.[183] For House, too, "public opinion comes nearer being right than the opinions of the leaders of a country."[184]

Richelieu warned Louis XIII that the king who permits the powerful to oppress the weak destroys himself. This conviction was, perhaps, dictated more by Richelieu's desire to hold the nobility in check than by more humane impulses.[185] In England, Bacon held that a powerful state must rest on a prosperous people, and his contemporaries found no difficulty in acknowledging that he was both an "indefatigable servant of the King and a most earnest lover of the Public."[186] Bacon's predecessors and contemporaries failed to note one curb on conscienceless men in high places to which Bacon drew particular attention: those who know how to stack the cards do not always know how to play them.

Lord Shang and Han Fei Tzu, generally viewed as Chinese Machiavellis, were no less persuaded of the importance of cultivating the people than their Renaissance counterpart. "A country where there are no dissatisfied people," said Lord Shang, "is called a strong country."[187] Despite his legalist label and his great respect for the controlling influence of law, Lord Shang reminded his prince that reforming the people goes deeper than merely issuing commands; the good example of the ruler is more important.[188] Laws should take into account customs and should not be established without examining the condition of the people.[189] The aim of punishment is to abolish punishment. When this has been achieved both love and hate will have become pure, which is to say that love will not be unjustly used to promote the advancement of friends and family nor hate to injure the welfare of others.[190]

---

[183]Machiavelli, *The Discourses*, p. 263.
[184]House, vol. 4, p. 235.
[185]Church, p. 33.
[186]Bacon, *Selected Writings*, p. xxviii.
[187]Shang, p. 205.
[188]Ibid., p. 27.
[189]Ibid., p. 238.
[190]Ibid., pp. 324–325. The following story told by Han Fei Tzu presumably illustrates what Lord Shang meant by a "pure" hatred. "Chieh Hu recommended [his enemy] Hsing Pai-liu to the governorship of Shang-tang. Liu went to thank him and said: 'You have forgiven me my fault. How dare I not repeat bows to you?' In reply Hu said: 'To raise you is a public matter; to hate you is a private affair. You had better go. My hatred for you remains the same as before.'" Han Fei Tzu, vol. 2, p. 83.

Han Fei Tzu was no less positive: "Though you have the wisdom of Yao but have no support of the masses of people, you cannot accomplish any great achievement."[191] In this, Han Fei Tzu and Lord Shang represented a strong tradition in the political thought of China. For the Confucian writers and Motse, political power, both domestic and foreign, rests on the ability to attract people by providing better living conditions than they can find in neighboring states. When the king is just and does not find pleasure in killing men, said Mencius, people will flock to him as surely as water flows downward. When a ruler asked Mencius what was required to attain imperial sway, Mencius replied: "The love and protection of the people; with this there is no power which can prevent a ruler from attaining it."[192] If you cannot make those who are close to you friendly, said Motse, there is just no use in trying to attract those who live at a distance.[193] Even after the unification of the Chinese states, this theme continued to be expressed by the Confucian literati. When rulers cultivate righteousness to gain the people's confidence, then nearby folk will lovingly flock to them and distant people joyfully submit to their authority. Therefore, the master conqueror does not fight; the expert warrior needs no soldiers.[194] This is in accordance with Confucius' definition of good government: "The near are happy and the distant attracted."[195]

Artistotle's *Politics* expresses similar convictions. If oligarchies and aristocracies endure, this is not because of any stability inherent in these forms of government but because of fair treatment. In an oligarchy great care should be taken of the poor, lucrative offices should be given to them, and members of the wealthy class who insult them should be severely punished.[196] In India, Kautilya warned against arousing popular fury, thus echoing a sentiment expressed in *The Panchatantra:*

---

[191]Han Fei Tzu, vol. 1, p. 259.

[192]Legge, vol. 2, p. 138.

[193]Motse, p. 6.

[194]*Discourses on Salt and Iron*, p. 4.

[195]Confucius, *Analects*, XIII, 16. The Berlin Wall and the suppression by Communist regimes of the free movement of populations are contemporary instances of attempts to resist political forces "attracting those who are distant."

[196]Aristotle, *Politics*, bk. V, 1308^a and 1309^a.

Beware the populace enraged;
A crowd's a fearsome thing:
The ants devoured the giant snake
For all his quivering.[197]

The conviction that even the most arbitrary political power is only secure when it solicits and gains the support of the people was not infrequently associated with a view of political life that justified one standard of morality in personal matters and an entirely different one for affairs of state. *Raison d'état* or reasons of state security have to the present day provided rulers and statesmen with justification for actions that law and private morality usually condemn. Machiavelli's *The Prince* was attacked as a principal proponent of the proposition that morality was not a relevant consideration in the management of state affairs; it was desirable to have a reputation for morality but not to be hampered by it. To what extent Machiavelli was describing the common practices of princes or proposing and defending them has been a subject of sustained controversy that we can hardly enter into here, although it is worth noting that a certain ambiguity in his language was perhaps inevitable in a book written to appeal to a Medici. Perhaps, too, it is not irrelevant to point out that Aristotle whose moral good faith is not generally in question, also used the language of *pre*scription as well as *de*scription in giving an account of what tyrants do and should or need to do to maintain their rule.[198] Machiavelli's advice to the prince to simulate virtue differs little from similar advice given to tyrants by Aristotle, although perhaps Aristotle intended to recommend ways of simulating virtue that might make the tyrant more virtuous than he wished to be.

In India, the observance or disregard of moral standards in state behavior was reflected in two types of political systems—Dharma Shāstra which required righteousness in both the choice of ends and in the application of means, and Artha Shāstra that sought the attainment of ends without regard to the nature of the means that might have to be employed.[199] Kautilya's *Arthasastra* is the great exemplar of the second view.

---

[197]*The Panchatantra*, p. 326.
[198]Aristotle, *Politics*, bk. V, 1313^{b}.
[199]*Sources of Indian Tradition*, p. 237.

Botero, in his *Reason of State* and Frederick the Great in his *L'anti-Machiavel*, both laid claim, in opposition to Machiavelli, to restoring morality to state behavior, although in neither case do the contents of these works, and still less Frederick's own behavior, show pronounced deviations from positions attributed to Machiavelli.[200]

The political advisers of past ages were not particularly distinguished by their moral standards, but the vast possibilities for evil inherent in the authority of the prince and the great nobles of his realm placed a premium on trying to provide some *moral* restraints to guard against the dangers of arbitrary, personal rule. However, in time, attempts to mold or reform the prince were replaced by efforts to render him harmless through a greater diffusion of political power. Ultimately, democracy provided a means, not to reform the leader and his advisers, but to replace them if they became insupportable. Thus the possibility of rejecting a leader dissolved the earlier concern to create one.

The transition to universal suffrage produced other changes as well. In periods of autocratic rule it was understandable that in the political realm preoccupation with virtue should largely center on that of the political leader and his advisers in whose hands power was concentrated. In popular states, however, a new situation arose that was recognized by Montesquieu in his *Spirit of the Laws*: "A great deal of probity is not necessary in order for a monarchy or despotic government to maintain itself. The force of law in the first case or the raised arm of the prince in the other regulates everything. But in a popular state one additional mechanism is required—virtue. What I am saying is confirmed by all history. . . . When virtue vanishes, ambition enters in the hearts of some and avarice in the hearts of all. . . . Every citizen is like a slave escaped from his master. . . . What were once called rules are now called inconveniences. What was once called respect is now called fear. . . . Formerly the property of private individuals created the public treasury, but now the public treasury becomes the patrimony of private individuals. The republic is a booty and its force is only the

[200]See, for example, Frederick's defense of breaking treaties, *L'anti-Machiavel*, p. 283.

power of some citizens and the lack of discipline of all. . . . A republic needs virtue, a monarchy honor, a despotism fear."[201]

With the increased power of the citizenry, its own virtue, then, as well as that of its leaders is at issue. Partly virtue is the moral obligation experienced in personal relations with family, friends, and strangers; partly it is the moral obligation of those who share a common corporate membership, and as a very special and important case of the latter, it is the obligations involved in membership in a political community, that is, it is *civic* virtue.

The growth of democracy gave to legislators and to legislation a central role in the rational direction of social life. Hume had approved the maxim that on principle every man should be held to be a knave. It was for the legislator by his laws to ensure that men's natural egoism was so directed as to induce their cooperation for the public good even against their own will. Bentham developed this theme into a science of legislation.[202]

Today the social planner, the policy analyst, and experts of many types, together with the legislator, rely almost exclusively on legal machinery and material incentives, and regard society largely as an assemblage of conflicting individual and group interests that, when properly constrained by law and administrative regulations, permit the realization of social plans.

We have already noted that only occasionally is there some recognition by the policy analyst that charisma or *virtù*, that is, good leadership, is an indispensable ingredient of many social programs, and that the design of these programs requires that the quality of the available leadership be taken into account or even, if necessary (and possible), changed. A parallel situation exists with respect to civic virtue; it is only fleetingly, if at all, acknowledged by the designers and managers of social programs to be an essential element in planned social action. The moral failings of political leaders and the injustices inherent in varying degrees in any social system have made it easy not only for the citizenry at large, but also for social planners and policy analysts to neglect the status of the citizenry's own public morality and its significance for the design and successful implementation of policy in many spheres. Even

[201] Montesquieu, *De l'esprit des lois*, pp. 20–22 and 26.
[202] Halévy, pp. 14–34.

so brutal a planner as Lord Shang had not supposed that in the long run one ought to try to run a society by rewards and punishments alone, and had recognized the need to produce, finally, an inbred discipline and civic virtue that avoided exclusive reliance on the enticements of rewards and the threat of punishment. Today civic virtue or public morality rarely enters either as a feature whose level in different population sectors must be taken account of in the design of social plans, or even less as an important asset subject to development and utilization in the service of social planning.

The foregoing tendencies are, no doubt, associated with the absence of strong political leadership, since such leadership generally assumes some responsibility and achieves some success, for good or evil, in mobilizing popular sentiments. The world energy crisis will no doubt give political leaders the opportunity, perhaps impose the necessity, to show that the mobilization of civic sentiments is an important component of policy planning. Today it is only in time of war or in the face of threats of grave disaster that civic sentiments are thought in the United States to be relevant. This increases for the adviser and the leader the difficulties of directing a complex society, and these often outrun the adviser's and leader's capacity for understanding and calculation. When uncertainty and perplexity reign, the safest course, said Montaigne, is simply to choose that option that accords most with uprightness and justice. The shortest road is the straightest road, [203] a view echoed by Colonel House when he said that the best politics was simply to do what was right; and echoed, too, by Samuel Taylor Coleridge when he praised "that fortunate inconsequence of our nature which permits the heart to rectify the errors of the understanding."[204]

---

[203]Montaigne, vol. 1, p. 171.
[204]Coleridge, *Biographia Literaria*, p. 114.

Bibliography

Adams, John. *Diary and Autobiography*. Ed. L. H. Butterfield. Vol. 3. *Diary 1782–1804; Autobiography Part One to October 1776. (The Adams Papers,* series I, Diaries.) Cambridge: Harvard University Press, The Belknap Press, 1961.

Adenauer, Konrad. *Memoirs 1945–53*. Translated by Beate Ruhm von Oppen. Chicago: Henry Regnery Company, 1966.

Aesop. *Fables*. Translated by S. A. Handford. Harmondsworth: Penguin Books, 1954.

Allen, Henry. "Consultants Have All the Answers," *Los Angeles Times*, September 2, 1973.

L'anti-Machiavel. See Frédéric II.

Appollonius of Rhodes. *The Voyage of Argo*. Translated by E. V. Rieu. Harmondsworth: Penguin Books, 1959.

Aquinas, St. Thomas. *On Kingship*. Translated by Gerald B. Phelan. Rev. by I. Th. Eschmann. Toronto: The Pontifical Institute of Medieval Studies, 1949.

Aristotle. "Ethica Nicomachea," *The Works of Aristotle*. Translated and edited by W. D. Ross. Vol. 9. London: Oxford University Press, 1915.

———. "Politica," *The Works of Aristotle*. Translated by Benjamin Jowett. Vol. 10. Ed. W. D. Ross. Oxford: The Clarendon Press, 1921.

———. "Rhetorica," *The Works of Aristotle*. Translated by W. Rhys Roberts. Vol. 11. Ed. W. D. Ross. Oxford: The Clarendon Press, 1924.

Armstrong, Edward. *The Emperor Charles V.* Vol. 2. 2d ed. London: Macmillan, 1910.
Arrian. *The Indica*. Translated by E. J. Chinnock. (*The Greek Historians*, vol. 2.) New York: Random House, 1942.
Ashton, Robert, ed. *James I by His Contemporaries*. London: Hutchinson, 1969.
Aubrey's Brief Lives. Ed. Oliver Lawson Dick. Ann Arbor: The University of Michigan Press, 1957.
Ayling, Stanley. *George the Third*. New York: Knopf, 1972.
Bacon, Francis. *Essays*. New York: Hurst, 1883.
———. *Selected Writings*. Introduction and notes by Hugh G. Dick. Eds. James Spedding, R. L. Ellis, and D. D. Heath. London, 1857–74. New York: Random House, The Modern Library, 1955.
———. "History of the Reign of King Henry VII" in *The Works of Francis Bacon*. Ed. James Spedding, et al. Vol. XI. Boston: Houghton Mifflin, 1900.
———. *The Works*. Vol. II. Philadelphia: 1859.
Bailey, Thomas A. *The Art of Diplomacy: The American Experience*. New York: Appleton-Century-Crofts, 1968.
Bengtson, Hermann. *Griechische Geschichte: von den Anfängen bis in die römische Kaiserzeit*. 3d ed. Munich: Beck, 1965.
Benoist, Charles. *Le machiavélisme de l'antimachiavel*. Librairie Plon. Paris: Plon-Nourrit et cie., 1915.
Birkenhead, Frederick, second Earl of. *The Professor and the Prime Minister: The Official Life of Professor F. A. Lindemann, Viscount Cherwell*. Boston: Houghton Mifflin, 1962.
Bismarck the Man and the Statesman, Being the Reflections and Reminiscences of Otto, Prince von Bismarck Written and Dictated by Himself after His Retirement from Office. Translated under supervision of A. J. Butler. 4 vols. New York: Harper & Brothers, 1899.
Bodde, Derk. *China's First Unifier: A Study of the Ch'in Dynasty as Seen in the Life of Li Ssu (280?–208 B.C.)*. Leiden: E. J. Brill, 1938.
———, tr. *Statesman, Patriot, and General in Ancient China: Three "Shih Chi" Biographies of the Ch'in Dynasty (255–206 B.C.)*. New Haven (Conn.): American Oriental Society, 1940.
Boethius. *The Consolation of Philosophy*. New York: Random House, The Modern Library, 1943.
Bontems, Claude, Raybaud, Léon-Pierre, and Brancourt, Jean-Pierre. *Le Prince dans la France des XVIe and XVIIe siècles*. Paris: Presses Universitaires de France, 1965.
The Book of Lord Shang, A Classic of the Chinese School of Law. Translated by J. J. L. Duyvendak. London: Arthur Probsthain, 1928.
Born, Lester Kruger. "The Perfect Prince: A Study in Thirteenth- and Fourteenth-Century Ideals," *Speculum*, III (4), October 1928a, pp. 470–504.
———. "Erasmus on Political Ethics: The Institutio Principis Christiani," *Political Science Quarterly*, XLIII (4), December 1928b, pp. 520–543.

———. 1965. See Erasmus. *The Education of a Christian Prince.*

Botero, Giovanni. *The Reason of State*. Translated by P. J. and D. P. Waley. London: Routledge & Kegan Paul, 1956.

Bradshaw, Kenneth, and Pring, David. *Parliament and Congress*. Austin: University of Texas Press, 1972.

Brooke, John. *King George III*. London: Constable, 1972.

Browne, Sir Thomas. "Religio Medici," in *The Consolation of Philosophy*. New York: Random House, The Modern Library, 1943.

La Bruyère. *Les caractères ou les moeurs de ce siècle*. Paris: Les Editions Bordas, 1969.

Buber, Martin. *Tales of the Hasidim: The Early Masters*. Translated by Olga Marx. New York: Schocken Books, 1961.

Budé, Guillaume. "L'institution du prince," *Le Prince dans la France des XVIe et XVIIe siècles*. See Bontems.

von Bülow, Bernhard. *Memoirs*. Translated by F. A. Voigt. 4 vols. Boston: Little, Brown, 1931–1932.

Callières, François de. *On the Manner of Negotiating with Princes*. Translated by A. F. Whyte. Boston: Houghton Mifflin, 1919.

Carr, Raymond. *Spain: 1808–1939*. Oxford: The Clarendon Press, 1966.

Cassels, Lavender. *The Struggle for the Ottoman Empire*. New York: Thomas Y. Crowell Company, 1967.

Chamfort. *Maximes et pensées, caractères et anecdotes*. Paris: Garnier-Flammarion, 1968.

Chan-kuo Ts'e. Translated by J. I. Crump, Jr. Oxford: The Clarendon Press, 1970.

Chuang Tzu. See Waley, Arthur.

Church, William F., ed. *The Impact of Absolutism in France: National Experience under Richelieu, Mazarin, and Louis XIV*. New York: John Wiley, 1969.

Cicero, Marcus Tullius. *On the Commonwealth*. Translated by George Holland Sabine and Stanley Barney Smith. Columbus: The Ohio State University Press, 1929.

———. *De Officiis*. Translated by Walter Miller. London: William Heinemann, The Loeb Classical Library, 1938.

———. *De Re Publica, De Legibus*. Translated by Clinton Walker Keyes. London: William Heinemann, The Loeb Classical Library, 1951.

———. *De Senectute, De Amicitia, De Divinatione*. Translated by William Armistead Falconer. London: William Heinemann, The Loeb Classical Library, 1953.

Coleridge, Samuel Taylor. *Biographia Literaria*. London: J. M. Dent, Everyman's Library, 1906.

Commynes, Philippe de. *Memoirs: The Reign of Louis XI*. Translated by Michael Jones. Harmondsworth: Penguin Books, 1972.

Comprehensive Discussions in the White Tiger Hall. See *Po Hu T'ung*.

Confucius. *The Analects or the Conversations of Confucius with his Disciples and Certain Others*. Translated by William Edward Soothill. Oxford University Press. London: Humphrey Milford, 1937.

Couvreur, Séraphin. *Les annales de la Chine*. Paris: Cathasia, 1950.
Cronin, Thomas E., and Greenberg, Sanford D., eds. *The Presidential Advisory System*. New York: Harper & Row, 1969.
Crump, J. I., Jr. 1970. See *Chan-kuo Ts'e*.
———. *Intrigues: Studies of the Chan-kuo Ts'e*. Ann Arbor: The University of Michigan Press, 1964.
"The Development of Social Thought and Institutions: War and Reorientation," *Encyclopedia of the Social Sciences*, 1937, I, pp. 189–228.
Devlin, Patrick. *Too Proud to Fight: Woodrow Wilson's Neutrality*. New York: Oxford University Press, 1975.
Diplomacy for the 70s, United States Department of State publication 8551, Washington, D.C., 1970.
Discourses on Salt and Iron, A Debate on State Control of Commerce and Industry in Ancient China. Translated and edited by Esson McDowell Gale. Leiden: E. J. Brill, 1931.
Eiduson, Bernice T. "Scientists as Advisors and Consultants in Washington," *Bulletin of the Atomic Scientists*, XXII (8), October 1966, pp. 26–31.
Emerson, Ralph Waldo. *The Dial*, Vol. IV, no. 1, July 1843.
The Epic of Gilgamesh. Translated by N. K. Sandars. Rev. ed., 1964. Harmondsworth: Penguin Books, 1971.
Epictetus. *The Discourses and Manual*. Translated with introduction and notes by P. E. Matheson. 2 vols. London: Oxford University Press, 1916.
Erasmus, Desiderius. *The Education of a Christian Prince*. Translated with an introduction by Lester K. Born. New York: Octagon Books, 1965.
Eyck, Erich. "Bismarck" in *From Metternich to Hitler*. Ed. W. N. Medlicott. New York: Barnes & Noble, 1963.
Fagniez, G. C. *Le Père Joseph et Richelieu*. 2 vols. Paris: Hachette, 1894.
Fallaci, Oriana. Interview, reprinted in the *Los Angeles Times*, December 30, 1973.
Ferguson, Adam. *An Essay on the History of Civil Society*. 3d ed. London: 1768.
Finley, M. I. *The Use and Abuse of History*. London: Chatto and Windus, 1975.
Fisher, Herbert A. L. *Political Prophecies*. Oxford: The Clarendon Press, 1919.
Fleisher, Martin. "A Passion for Politics: The Vital Core of the World of Machiavelli" in *Machiavelli and the Nature of Political Thought*. Ed. Martin Fleisher. New York: Atheneum, 1972.
Frédéric II. *L'anti-Machiavel. (Studies on Voltaire and the Eighteenth Century* series, ed. Theodore Besterman, vol. V.) Geneva: Institut et Musée Voltaire, Les Délices, 1958.
de Gaulle, Charles. *The Edge of the Sword*. Translated by Gerard Hopkins. New York: Criterion Books, 1960.
George, Alexander L. and George, Juliette L. *Woodrow Wilson and Colonel House*. New York: John Day, 1956.

Gilbert, Allan H. *Machiavelli's Prince and Its Forerunners*. Durham (N.C.): Duke University Press, 1938.

Gilbert, Felix. *Machiavelli and Guicciardini*. Princeton: Princeton University Press, 1965.

Gilgamesh. See *The Epic of Gilgamesh*.

Gilmore, Myron P. *Humanists and Jurists: Six Studies in the Renaissance*. Cambridge: Harvard University Press, The Belknap Press, 1963.

Giraldus Cambrensis. *The Autobiography of Giraldus Cambrensis*. Edited and translated by H. E. Butler. London: Jonathan Cape, 1937.

———. *The Conquest of Ireland* in *The Historical Works of Giraldus Cambrensis*. Translated by Thomas Forester. Revised and edited by Thomas Wright. London: 1863.

———. *The Itinerary Through Wales. Description of Wales*. Translated by Sir Richard Colt Hoare, 1806. London: J. M. Dent, Everyman's Library, 1908.

Goldhamer, Herbert. *The Foreign Powers in Latin America*. Princeton: Princeton University Press, 1972.

Gooch, G. P. *Political Thought in England from Bacon to Halifax*. London: Thornton Butterworth, 1914.

Gorham, William. "A Social Report and Social Policy Advisers," in *The Presidential Advisory System*. See Cronin and Greenberg.

Gracián, Balthasar. *The Art of Worldly Wisdom*. Translated by Joseph Jacobs. New York: Frederick Ungar Publishing, n.d.

Grimaldus, Laurentius. *The Counsellor*, Exactly Pourtraited in Two Bookes, Written in Latin by Laurentius Grimaldus and Consecrated to the Honour of the Polonian Empyre, Newlie translated into English, London, 1598.

Guicciardini, Francesco. *History of Italy and History of Florence*. Translated by Cecil Grayson. Edited and abridged by John R. Hale. New York: Twayne Publishers, 1964.

———. *Maxims and Reflections*. Translated by Mario Domandi. Philadelphia: University of Pennsylvania Press, 1965.

Hale, John R. See Guicciardini, *History of Italy . . .*

Haines, J. *The Politics of Power*. London: Cape, 1977.

Halévy, Elie. *The Growth of Philosophic Radicalism*. Translated by Mary Morris. New York: Macmillan, 1928.

Han Fei Tzu. *The Complete Works*. Translated by W. K. Liao. 2 vols. London: Arthur Probsthain, vol. 1, 1939; vol. 2, 1959.

Harbison, E. Harris. "Machiavelli's 'Prince' and More's 'Utopia,'" in *Facets of the Renaissance*. Ed. William H. Werkmeister. Los Angeles: The University of Southern California Press, 1959.

Harris, Seymour E. *The Economics of the Political Parties*. New York: Macmillan, 1962.

Harrod, R. F. *The Prof: A Personal Memoir of Lord Cherwell*. London: Macmillan, 1959.

Heller, Walter W. "Economic Policy Advisers" in *The Presidential Advisory System*. See Cronin and Greenberg.
Herodotus. *The Persian Wars*. Translated by George Rawlinson. (*The Greek Historians*, vol. 1.) New York: Random House, 1942.
Hesiod. *Works and Days*. Translated by Hugh G. Evelyn-White. In Hesiod, *The Homeric Hymns and Homerica*. London: William Heinemann, The Loeb Classical Library, 1926.
"History of the Forty Vezirs" in *Turkish Literature*. Translated by Epiphanius Wilson. Rev. ed. New York: P. F. Collier, 1901.
Hobbes, Thomas. *Leviathan*. London: J. M. Dent, Everyman's Library, 1914.
Holinshed, Raphael. *The Chronicles:* newly augmented 1586, vol. 3. London: 1587.
The Holstein Papers. Vol. 1: *Memoirs and Political Observations*. Eds. Norman Rich and M. H. Fisher. Cambridge: Cambridge University Press, 1955.
Homer, *The Iliad.*
House. See Seymour, Charles (ed.).
House, Edward M. [Anonymous.] *Philip Dru: Administrator.* New York: B. H. Huebsch, 1912.
Hsüntze. *The Works*. Translated by Homer H. Dubbs. London: Arthur Probsthain, 1928.
Hughes. See *Tso Chuan*.
Huxley, Aldous. *Grey Eminence*; a study in religion and politics. New York: Harper & Brother, 1941.
Ibn Iskandar. *A Mirror for Princes*. Translated by Reuben Levy. New York: E. P. Dutton, 1951.
Issawi. See Ibn Khaldun.
James VI. *The Basilicon Doron*. Edited by James Craigie. 2 vols. Edinburgh: William Blackwood & Sons, The Scottish Text Society, vol. 1, 1944; vol. 2, 1950.
Joinville, Jean Sire de. "Chronicle of the Crusade of St. Lewis," in *Memoirs of the Crusades*. Translated by Frank T. Marzials. London: J. M. Dent, Everyman's Library, 1908.
Juan Manuel, Don. *Count Lucanor*. Translated by James York, M.D. London: 1868.
Juvenal. *The Sixteen Satires*. Translated by Peter Green. Harmondsworth: Penguin Books, 1967.
Kangle, R. P. See *The Kautilya Arthasastra, Part II.*
The Kautilya Arthasastra, Part II. Translated by R. P. Kangle. 2d ed. (University of Bombay Studies, Sanskrit, Prakrit, and Pali, no. 2.) Bombay: University of Bombay, 1972.
Kautilya's Arthasastra. Translated by R. Shamasastry. 8th ed. Mysore: Mysore Printing and Publishing House, 1967.
Ibn Khaldun. *The Muqaddimah, An Introduction to History*. Translated by Franz Rosenthal. 3 vols. New York: Pantheon Books, 1958.

———. *An Arab Philosophy of History: Selections from the Prolegomena of Ibn Khaldun*. Translated by Charles Issawi. London: John Murray, 1950.

A King's Lessons in Statecraft: Louis XIV: Letters to His Heirs. Translated by Herbert Wilson. Introduction and Notes by Jean Longnon. New York: Albert & Charles Boni, 1925.

The King's Mirror. Translated by Laurence Marcellus Larson. (Scandinavian Monographs, vol. III.) New York: The American-Scandinavian Foundation, 1917.

Kissinger, Henry A. *A World Restored: Metternich, Castlereagh, and The Problems of Peace 1812–1822*. Boston: Houghton Mifflin, 1957.

———. *The Necessity for Choice: Prospects of American Foreign Policy*. New York: Harper & Brothers, 1960.

———. Interview. Department of State *Bulletin*, November 11, 1974, pp. 629–642.

Kraft, Joseph. "The Washington Lawyers" in *The Presidential Advisory System*. See Cronin and Greenberg.

Laiglesia, F. de. *Estudios Históricos (1515–1555)*. Vol. 1. Madrid: Imprenta clásica española, 1918.

Landtman, Gunnar. *The Origin of the Inequality of the Social Classes*. Chicago: University of Chicago Press, 1938.

Langeron, Roger. *Decazes: Ministre du roi*. Paris: Librairie Hachette, 1960.

Langland, William. *Piers the Ploughman*. Translated into modern English by J. F. Goodridge. Rev. ed. Harmondsworth: Penguin Books, 1966.

Lasswell, Harold D. "Policy Sciences," *International Encyclopedia of the Social Sciences*, 1968, XII, 181–189.

———. *Politics: Who Gets What, When, How*. New York: McGraw-Hill, Whittlesey House, 1936.

Lasswell, Harold D., and Kaplan, Abraham. *Power and Society: A Framework for Political Inquiry*. New Haven: Yale University Press, 1950.

Legge, James. *The Chinese Classics*. Vol. II: *The Works of Mencius*. Oxford: The Clarendon Press, 1895.

Leites, Nathan. *A Study of Bolshevism*. Glencoe (Ill.): The Free Press, 1953.

Lerner, Daniel, and Lasswell, Harold D., eds. *The Policy Sciences: Recent Developments in Scope and Method*. Stanford (Calif.): Stanford University Press, 1951.

The Letters of the Younger Pliny. Translated by Betty Radice. Baltimore: Penguin Books, 1963.

Lie tseu. *Le vrai classique du vide parfait*. Translated into French by Benedykt Grynpas. (Collection UNESCO d'oeuvres représentatives.) Paris: Librairie Gallimard, 1961.

Lincoln, Abraham. *The Collected Works*. 8 vols. Ed. Roy P. Basler. New Brunswick (N.J.): Rutgers University Press, 1953.

Louis XIV. See *A King's Lessons in Statecraft*.

Lybyer, Albert Howe. *The Government of the Ottoman Empire in the Time of Suleiman the Magnificent*. Cambridge: Harvard University Press, 1913.

Machiavel. *Le Prince, suivi de Choix de lettres*. Translated into French by Jean Anglade. Paris: Librairie Générale Française, 1972.

Machiavelli, Niccolò. *The Chief Works and Others*. Translated by Allan Gilbert. 3 vols. Durham (N.C.): Duke University Press, 1965.

———. *The Prince and The Discourses. The Prince* translated by Luigi Ricci, rev. by E. R. P. Vincent; *The Discourses* translated by Christian E. Detmold. New York: Random House, The Modern Library, 1940.

———. *L'art de la guerre* in *Oeuvres complètes* (Bibliothèque de la Pléiade). Paris: Éditions Gallimard, 1952. pp. 723–910.

Maimonides, Moses. *The Guide for the Perplexed*. Translated by M. Friedländer. 2d ed., rev. New York: Dover Publications, 1956.

Mannheim, Karl. *Ideology and Utopia: An Introduction to the Sociology of Knowledge*. New York: Harcourt, Brace and Company, 1936.

Manuel. See Juan Manuel.

Marcellinus, Ammianus. *Julian the Apostate*. Translated by Philemon Holland. London: Blackie & Son, 1906.

Margouliès, G., ed. *Anthologie raisonnée de la littérature chinoise*. Paris: Payot, 1948.

von Martin, Alfred. *The Sociology of the Renaissance*. Translated by W. L. Luetkens. New York: Oxford University Press, 1944.

May, Ernest R. *"Lessons" of the Past: The Use and Misuse of History in American Foreign Policy*. New York: Oxford University Press, 1973.

Meinecke, Friedrich. *Machiavellism*. Translated by Douglas Scott. London: Routledge and Kegan Paul, 1957.

Melnik, Constantin, and Leites, Nathan. *The House Without Windows: France Selects a President*. Translated from the French by Ralph Manheim. Evanston (Ill.): Row, Peterson and Company, 1958.

Memoirs of Prince Metternich, 1773–1835. 5 vols. Translated by Mrs. Alexander Napier. Ed. Prince Richard Metternich. London: Richard Bentley & Son, 1880–1882.

Méthivier, Hubert. *Le siècle de Louis XIII*. 2d ed. Paris: Presses Universitaires de France, 1967.

Metternich. See *Memoirs of Prince Metternich . . .*

Miller, Merle. *Plain Speaking*. New York: Berkley Publishing, 1974.

Moley, Raymond. *27 Masters of Politics*. New York: Funk & Wagnalls, 1949.

Molière. *Oeuvres Complètes*. Vol. 1. (Bibliothèque de la Pléiade.) Paris: Librairie Gallimard, 1956.

Montaigne. *The Essays*. Translated by George B. Ives. 4 vols. Cambridge: Harvard University Press, 1925.

Montesquieu. *Un carnet inédit: Le Spicilège*. Paris: Flammarion, 1944.

———. *De l'esprit des lois*. Paris: Garnier Frères, n.d.

More, Sir Thomas. "Utopia" in *Ideal Commonwealths*. Rev. ed. Ed. Henry Moreley. New York: P. F. Collier, 1901.

Morgenthau, Hans J. "Henry Kissinger, Secretary of State," *Encounter*, November 1974, pp. 57–61.

Motse. *The Ethical and Political Works*. Translated by Yi-Pao Mei. London: Arthur Probsthain, 1929.

Neustadt, Richard E. *Presidential Power, The Politics of Leadership*. New York: John Wiley, 1960.

Nicolson, Harold. *King George the Fifth: His Life and Reign*. London: Constable, 1952.

Norman, A.V.B. *The Medieval Soldier*. New York: Thomas Y. Crowell, 1971.

Operations Research, 19 (5), September 1971, pp. 1123–1258.

Operations Research, 20 (1), January–February 1972, pp. 205–244.

The Panchatantra. Translated by Arthur W. Ryder. Chicago: The University of Chicago Press, 1925.

"Parkinson Looks at Cabinet Governments," *The Economist*, November 3, 1956, pp. 395–397.

Pascal's Pensées. Translated by W. F. Trotter. Introduction by T. S. Eliot. New York: E. P. Dutton, 1958.

Penn, William. *The Peace of Europe: The Fruits of Solitude*. London: J. M. Dent, Everyman's Library, 1915.

Les penseurs grecs avant Socrate: de Thalès de Milet à Prodicos. Translated by Jean Voilquin. Paris: Garnier-Flammarion, 1964.

Plato. *The Dialogues*. Translated by B. Jowett. 2 vols. 3d ed. New York: Random House, 1937.

Pliny. See *The Letters of the Younger Pliny*.

Plutarch's Lives. The "Dryden Plutarch." Vol. 1. Revised by Arthur Hugh Clough. London: J. M. Dent, Everyman's Library, 1910.

Plutarch. *Moralia*. Vols. 5 and 10. Translated by F. C. Babbitt. London: William Heinemann, The Loeb Classical Library, 1936.

Po Hu T'ung, The Comprehensive Discussions in the White Tiger Hall. 2 vols. Translated by Tjan Tjoe Som. Leiden: E. J. Brill, vol. 1, 1949; vol. 2, 1952.

Polybius. *The Histories*. Translated from the text of F. Hultsch by Evelyn S. Shuckburgh. 2 vols. Bloomington: Indiana University Press, 1962.

Ratcliffe, Alexander L. "Die militärpolitische Lage am Jahresende," *Wehrkunde*, XVI (12), December 1967.

Richelieu, Cardinal de. *Maximes d'état et fragments politiques*. Ed. Gabriel Hanotaux. Paris: Imprimerie Nationale, 1880.

———. *The Political Testament of Cardinal Richelieu*. Translated by Henry Bertram Hill. Madison: The University of Wisconsin Press, 1961.

———. *Testament Politique*. Paris: Robert Laffont, 1947.

Rivarol. *Journal politique national*. Paris: Union Générale d'Éditions, 1964.

La Rochefoucauld. *Oeuvres Complètes*. (Bibliothèque de la Pléiade.) Paris: Librairie Gallimard, 1957.

Rousseau, Jean-Jacques. "A Discourse on the Arts and Sciences" in *The Social Contract and Discourses*. London: J. M. Dent, Everyman's Library, 1913.

Runciman, Steven. *Byzantine Civilization*. New York: Meridian Books, 1958.

Rusk, Dean. "The President," *Foreign Affairs*, April 1960, pp. 353–369.

Sarton, George. *Introduction to the History of Science*. Vol. II: From Rabbi Ben Ezra to Roger Bacon. Baltimore: Williams & Wilkins, 1931.

Sauvigny, Guillaume de Bertier. *Metternich and His Times*. Translated by Peter Ryde. London: Darton, Longman & Todd, 1962.

Scarborough, Reverend W. *A Collection of Chinese Proverbs*. Revised and enlarged by C. Wilfred Allan. 2d ed. New York: Paragon Book Reprint, 1964.

Schlesinger, Arthur M., Jr. *The Age of Roosevelt: The Coming of the New Deal*. Boston: Houghton Mifflin, 1959.

———. *A Thousand Days: John F. Kennedy in the White House*. Boston: Houghton Mifflin, 1965.

Seneca. *Letters from a Stoic*. Translated by Robin Campbell. Baltimore: Penguin Books, 1969.

Seymour, Charles, ed. *The Intimate Papers of Colonel House*. 4 vols. Boston: Houghton Mifflin, 1926–1928.

Shamasastry. See *Kautilya's Arthasastra*.

Shang. See *The Book of Lord Shang . . .*

Sherwood, Robert E. *Roosevelt and Hopkins*. New York: Harper & Row, 1948.

The Shu Ching. See *The Shu King*.

The Shu King or the Chinese Historical Classic. Translated by Walter Gorn Old. London: 1904.

Snow, C. P. *Science and Government*. Cambridge: Harvard University Press, 1961.

Sophocles. *Antigone*. Translated by R. C. Jebb. (*The Complete Greek Drama*, vol. 1.) New York: Random House, 1938.

Sorensen, Theordore C. *Kennedy*. New York: Harper & Row, 1965.

———. *The Kennedy Legacy*. New York: Macmillan, 1969.

Sources of Chinese Tradition. Compiled by Wm. Theodore de Bary, Wing-tsit Chan, Burton Watson. New York: Columbia University Press, 1960.

Sources of Indian Tradition. Compiled by Wm. Theodore de Bary, Stephen Hay, Royal Weiler, Andrew Yarrow. New York: Columbia University Press, 1958.

Spengler, Oswald. *The Decline of the West*. Translated by Charles Francis Atkinson. London: George Allen & Unwin, 1926.

Spiegel, Gabrielle M. "Political U'ility in Medieval Historiography," *History and Theory*, XIV(3), 1975, pp. 314–325.

Suetonius, Gaius. *The Twelve Caesars*. Translated by Robert Graves. Harmondsworth: Penguin Books, 1957.

Sun Tzu on the Art of War. Translated by Lionel Giles. London: 1910.

Sussmann, Leila A. *Dear FDR: A Study of Political Letter-Writing*. Totowa (N.J.): The Bedminster Press, 1963.

Swift, Jonathan. *Gulliver's Travels*. London: Oxford University Press, 1919.

Tacitus. *The Complete Works*. Translated by Alfred John Church and William Jackson Brodribb. Ed. Moses Hadas. New York: Random House, The Modern Library, 1942.

Thomas, Norman C., and Wolman, Harold L. "Policy Formulation in the Institutionalized Presidency: The Johnson Task Forces" in *The Presidential Advisory System*. See Cronin and Greenberg.

Thomasius, Christian. "Erfindung der Wissenschaften anderer Menschen Gemüt zu erkennen" in F. Brüggeman (ed.), *Aus der Frühzeit der deutschen Aufklärung*. Weimar: H. Böhlaus, 1928.

Thucydides. *The Peloponnesian War*. Translated by Richard Crawley. New York: Random House, The Modern Library, 1934.

Truman, Harry S. *Memoirs*. 2 vols. Garden City (N.Y.): Doubleday, vol. 1, 1955; vol. 2, 1956.

"Tso Chuan" in *Chinese Philosophy in Classical Times*. Edited and translated by E. R. Hughes. London: J. M. Dent, Everyman's Library, 1942.

Turner, Ralph V. *The King and His Courts*. Ithaca: Cornell University Press, 1968.

Vauvenargues. *Maximes et Réflexions*. Paris: Librairie Somogy, 1945.

da Vinci, Leonardo. *The Notebooks of Leonardo da Vinci*. Arranged, translated and introduced by Edward MacCurdy. New York: George Braziller, 1954.

The Voyage of Argo. See Appollonius.

Waddell, Helen. *The Wandering Scholars*. New York: Doubleday, Anchor Books, 1955.

Waley, Arthur. *Three Ways of Thought in Ancient China*. London: George Allen and Unwin, 1939.

Wang An Shih. See Williamson, H. R.

Weber, Max. *The Theory of Social and Economic Organization*. Ed. Talcott Parsons. Glencoe (Ill.): The Free Press, 1957.

Weisband, Edward, and Franck, Thomas M. *Resignation in Protest*. New York: Grossman Publishers, 1975.

Whicher, George F., trans. *The Goliard Poets*. A New Directions Book, 1949.

Williamson, H. R. *Wang An Shih*. 2 vols. London: Arthur Probsthain vol. I, 1935; vol. II, 1937.

Wilson, Edith Bolling. *My Memoir*. Indianapolis: Bobbs-Merrill, 1939.

Wolf, John B. *Louis XIV*. New York: W. W. Norton, 1968.

Wragg, H. *Letters Written in Wartime: XV–XIX Centuries*. London: Oxford University Press, 1915.

Wright, Arthur F. *Buddhism in Chinese History*. Stanford (Calif.): Stanford University Press, 1959.

Xenophon. *The Anabasis of Cyrus*. Translated by Henry G. Dakyns. (*The Greek Historians*, vol. 2.) New York: Random House, 1942.

———. *The Education of Cyrus*. Translated by Henry G. Dakyns. Revised by F. M. Stawell. London: J. M. Dent, Everyman's Library, 1914.

Index

The Rand Graduate Institute

PUBLISHED

Goldhamer, Herbert. *The Adviser*. New York: Elsevier-North Holland, Inc., 1978, a Rand Graduate Institute Book.

SELECTED RAND BOOKS ON POLICY ANALYSIS

Averch, Harvey A., John E. Koehler, and Frank H. Denton. *The Matrix of Policy in the Philippines*. New Jersey: Princeton University Press, 1971.

Fisher, Gene H. *Cost Considerations in Systems Analysis*. New York: American Elsevier Publishing Company, Inc., 1971.

Hirshleifer, Jack, James C. DeHaven, and Jerome W. Milliman. *Water Supply: Economics, Technology, and Policy*. Chicago, Illinois: University of Chicago Press, 1969.

Quade, E. S. *Analysis for Public Decisions*. New York: American Elsevier Publishing Company, Inc., 1975.